T0361872

The Theory of Futures Trading

First published in 1972, this book provides an important critical review on the theory of futures trading. B. A. Goss looks at the work and ideas of Keynes and Hicks on futures, and considers how these have also been developed by Kaldor. He discusses the evolution of the concept of hedging in the context of buying forward into the markets, and considers theories of market and individual equilibrium. Goss draws on the work of other economists in this field, including Stein, Telser, Peston and L. L. Johnson, in order to illustrate the development of theory in futures trading. The book includes fifteen figures that illustrate diagrammatically the concepts involved, and the concluding section contains a series of problems for examination by the student.

The Theory of Futures Trading

B. A. Goss

First published in 1972
by Routledge & Kegan Paul

This edition first published in 2013 by Routledge
2 Park Square, Milton Park, Abingdon, Oxon, OX14 4RN

Simultaneously published in the USA and Canada
by Routledge
711 Third Avenue, New York, NY 10017

Routledge is an imprint of the Taylor & Francis Group, an informa business

© 1972 B. A. Goss

Publisher's Note
The publisher has gone to great lengths to ensure the quality of this reprint but
points out that some imperfections in the original copies may be apparent.

Disclaimer
The publisher has made every effort to trace copyright holders and welcomes
correspondence from those they have been unable to contact.

A Library of Congress record exists under ISBN: 72195160

ISBN 13: 978-0-415-83520-6 (hbk)
ISBN 13: 978-0-203-38084-0 (ebk)

The Theory of Futures Trading

LONDON AND BOSTON
ROUTLEDGE & KEGAN PAUL

First published 1972
by Routledge & Kegan Paul Ltd
Broadway House, 68–74 Carter Lane,
London EC4V 5EL and
9 Park Street, Boston, Mass. 02108, U.S.A.
Printed in Great Britain by
Richard Clay (The Chaucer Press) Ltd
Bungay, Suffolk
© B. A. Goss, 1972
ISBN 0 7100 7217 1

General editor's introduction

Although all economists would agree that decision-making under risk and uncertainty was central to their subject, and that the role of special markets dealing with these phenomena are of vital importance in analysing the working of a decentralized economic system, there is no good elementary treatment available of this subject. In particular, while there is often a discussion of risk and uncertainty as such, this is not coupled with a discussion of its market consequences. The most important phenomena are, of course, the insurance industry on the one hand and, on the other, the subject of this book, forward markets and futures trading.

In this book, Dr Goss shows how these markets can be analysed using the basic tools of economic analysis. In particular, the student will be able to trace the connections between spot and futures prices, and to see what role futures and forward markets have in determining present price. He will then be able to go on to see how the existence of these markets helps to overcome the potential welfare loss due to risk and uncertainty.

The book fills a gap in the literature in an admirable way, and will enable teachers to introduce this topic into their lectures at the undergraduate and graduate level. In particular, they will be able to use it in an area in which techniques taught in other parts of the subject are relevant and helpful.

M. H. P.

Contents

Figures

Acknowledgments

Thanks are due to Basil Yamey for his careful supervision during my period as a graduate student at the London School of Economics, to Maurice Peston for his advice and criticism and to L. Roy Webb for discussion and advice during the initial stages of this work. None of these persons, however, is in any way responsible for the errors which remain.

Acknowledgment is also made to the editors of *Economica* for permission to reproduce a diagram from M. H. Peston and B. S. Yamey, 'Inter-Temporal Price Relationships with Forward Markets: A Method of Analysis', which appeared in the November 1960 issue of that journal; to the editors of the *Review of Economic Studies* for permission to reproduce two diagrams from L. L. Johnson, 'The Theory of Hedging and Speculation in Commodity Futures', which appeared on pp. 145–6 of vol. 27 (1959–60) of the *Review*; to the University of Chicago Press for permission to reproduce a diagram from L. G. Telser, 'Futures Trading and the Storage of Cotton and Wheat', *Journal of Political Economy*, vol. 66 (1958), p. 240; and to the editors, *Australian Economic Papers*, for permission to use material from B. A. Goss, 'A Note on the Storage Market Equilibria of Brennan and Telser', which appeared in the December 1970 issue of that journal.

ACKNOWLEDGMENTS

In addition, gratitude is expressed to Mrs Jean Earle and Miss Lesley Taskis who typed the manuscript, and to Miss Janine Blackley who drew the diagrams and assisted in checking the manuscript.

Introduction

Nature of futures trading

There are two current prices for any commodity: a price for delivery now, the spot price and a price for delivery at a later date, the forward price.

Consider the case of a farmer with a growing crop, with a period of production of, say, nine months; suppose that the current spot price is $10 per bushel. His risk is that the price of the commodity will fall before the crop is ready for delivery. If a buyer were to offer, say, $9.50 per bushel for delivery in nine months' time and the farmer accepts, the crop would be sold forward, and the farmer would have hedged his position against the risk of a price fall. That is, the farmer would have obtained certainty, and the price risk would now be borne by the buyer.

On the other hand, consider the case of a flour-miller who has contracted to deliver a quantity of flour in six months' time, at an agreed price. His risk is that the price of wheat will rise before he purchases his requirements, in, say, five months' time. If he were to purchase wheat forward currently at an agreed price, then the flour-miller would have hedged his position against the risk of a price rise in wheat. That is, he would have acquired certainty, and that risk would now be borne by the seller of the wheat.

1

Hedging, then, is defined as the activity of a trader who enters the forward market with a spot market commitment, and hence a spot market price risk, and who, by forward dealing, makes his position certain and transfers the risk to another party.

In the first example the farmer possessed the growing crop, i.e. he was 'short' in the forward market. He is thus said to be a short hedger. In the second example, the flour-miller sold forward flour which he did not possess; in terms of the wheat equivalent of that flour, he was 'short' in the spot market. He bought wheat forward, i.e. he was 'long' in the forward market for wheat, and is said to be a long hedger.

These examples, while being cases of forward trading, are not instances of futures trading. A future is a contract which refers to a specific later date, for a fixed quantity of the standard grade of a commodity. The future, rather than the commodity to which it refers, is the unit of trading. Delivery is possible, optional, but is seldom made. Futures market positions are usually closed out by reversal of the transaction.

The procedure for a short hedger, say a stockholder of wheat, who took his hedge in a wheat futures market, would be as follows:

At time t_0 the stockholder would buy wheat spot at a unit price of S_0, and would hedge by selling futures contracts for an equivalent quantity of wheat, at a unit price of F_0.

At t_1 he would sell the wheat spot at a price S_1, and would close out the futures market position by buying a quantity of futures (equal to the quantity initially sold) at a price F_1.

His total profit on the hedged position can be expressed as:

$$\text{(profit on spot) minus (loss on futures)}$$
$$= (S_1 - S_0) - (F_1 - F_0)$$
$$= (S_1 - F_1) - (S_0 - F_0), \tag{1}$$

which may be $\gtreqless 0$.

That is, a short hedger makes a profit if backwardation (a market term to describe a situation in which $S > F$) increases.

Equation (1) may be written as

$$(F_0 - S_0) - (F_1 - S_1), \qquad (2)$$

which may be $\gtrless 0$.

That is, short hedgers make a profit if contango (a market term to describe a situation in which $F > S$) declines.

If the price spread or 'basis' (the difference between S and F) remains constant, i.e. S and F move in the same direction and by the same amount, the profit on the hedged position is zero. The hedge is said to be perfect.

So a stockholder, initially facing the risk of a fall in the spot price, hedges by selling futures; his risk is now that the spot and futures prices will not move in parallel: he has substituted a basis risk for a price risk.

The hedge described above is a pure hedge: the trader sold a quantity of futures contracts equal to the quantity of wheat involved in his spot market commitment, neither more nor less. Such a trader will always hedge his spot market position, even if the spot price is expected to rise: a pure hedger is assumed not to back his expectations, or alternatively, not to have any expectations.

We may also consider the case of a long hedger who hedges in a futures market. For example, suppose a flour-miller sells flour forward at time t_0, at a price S_0. The price S_0 is assumed to be deflated by the cost of converting wheat to flour: that is, it refers to the commodity content of the finished product.[1] It is usually interpreted as the spot price of the wheat equivalent of the flour sold forward. The miller hedges by buying an equivalent quantity of wheat futures at price F_0.

At t_1 he buys wheat spot at the price S_1, and closes out his futures position by selling wheat futures at a price F_1. His profit on the hedged position is seen to be:

3

$$(S_0 - S_1) - (F_0 - F_1)$$
$$= (S_0 - F_0) - (S_1 - F_1) \quad (3)$$

or

$$= (F_1 - S_1) - (F_0 - S_0) \quad (4)$$

which may be $\gtreqless 0$.

Hence the long hedger is said to make a profit if backwardation declines (equation 3) or if contango increases (equation 4). So the short hedger's gain is said to be the long hedger's loss, and *vice versa*; and their actuals and futures transactions are of opposite sign. For these reasons the long hedger's position is often regarded as the negative or mirror image of that of the short hedger.

This is not strictly true, however, because the long hedger's actuals transaction at t_0 is a forward transaction, and 'S_0' in equation (3) is really a forward price.[2] It is therefore likely to be closer to F_0, than to the spot price at t_0: hence ('S_0' $- F_0$) in equation (3) cannot be interpreted as backwardation.

Pre-conditions for futures trading

The following would appear to be the necessary conditions for commodity futures trading to be possible. The first condition is that there must exist rigidities in production which give rise to spot market commitments, either on the long or on the short side of the market. Once such a commitment exists it can be avoided only at considerable cost to the party concerned. For example, a farmer with a growing crop is committed to harvesting and selling the crop. To avoid this commitment by destroying the crop would involve him in considerable loss. Similarly, a builder who has contracted to build a brick house is committed to buying bricks at some time in the future: to avoid this commitment he must give up the contract.

Second, the price of the commodity must fluctuate, or be

expected to fluctuate. Hence persons with a spot market commitment face a price risk. As a consequence of these first two conditions taken together there will be a demand for hedging facilities. It is conceivable that a futures market could exist without hedgers, that is with arbitrageurs and speculators alone.[3] Hedging activities, however, are regarded as an important part of futures trading in practice.[4]

The third condition is that the commodity must be homogeneous or, alternatively, it must be possible to specify a standard grade and to measure deviations from that grade. This condition is necessary if a futures exchange is to deal in a standardized contract. In some commodities there may be two or more standard contracts; for example, in copper at the London Metal Exchange there are three standard contracts: one each for Wirebars, Cathodes and Fire Refined. Frequently, however, trading tends to concentrate in one contract.

Discounts and premia are fixed by the exchange to correspond to grades of the commodity 'below' and 'above' the standard grade. If delivery of a non-standard grade is made, then this discount or premium is applied to the price of the contract at that time (maturity).

Fourth, delivery of the commodity must be possible under the contract. If this condition is fulfilled, then theoretically the price of a future at maturity will equal the spot price at that date; that is, maturity basis will be zero, because it will be a matter of indifference to a buyer of the actual commodity whether he purchases the commodity spot or purchases a future at maturity and obtains delivery. In practice, the maturity basis may not be zero; for example, the buyer may be a user of a particular grade and may be uncertain which grade will be delivered. The spot commodity may then command a premium over the maturing future.[5]

If this condition were not fulfilled, the price of a future at maturity would bear no necessary relation to the spot price at that date.[6]

The fifth condition is that storage of the commodity must be possible. In the absence of this condition, arbitrage of the type referred to in the section 'Categories of transaction' of this Introduction would not be possible. There would then be no necessary relationship between spot and futures prices before maturity.

The fourth and fifth conditions would appear to rule out the possibility of futures trading in services, because specific performance (i.e. 'delivery') cannot usually be legally insisted upon in the case of services, and storage of services is not possible.

Although the holding of stocks must be financed whether the commodity is the subject of futures trading or not, it would appear that futures trading requires that sufficient liquid funds be available to facilitate market settlement. This is the sixth condition.

Finally, it follows that in so far as hedgers are either net long or net short, there must be a speculative element present which is net short or net long respectively, to take up the balance of open positions.

Feasibility, however, is not the same thing as success. Although one may argue that all necessary conditions for futures trading are fulfilled, this is no guarantee that the market will be active. There appear to be three main reasons why this may not be so.[7] The first is that the contract may favour one side of the market, for example, with respect to commodity description, delivery provisions or the testing procedure for deliverable stocks. Second, if in the commercial market power is concentrated on one side of the market, and the futures contract merely reflects this concentration, there may be no incentive for the group holding the power to use the market. Third, one group of traders may be traditionally accustomed to a particular form of market arrangement, and may be unwilling to break that tradition.

Categories of transaction

The purpose of this section is to classify transactions into three categories, hedging, arbitrage and speculation, and to indicate the aims of each of these different types of transaction. This classification of transactions is conceptual only, and in practice any one operator, or any one market transaction may fall into two, or all three, categories simultaneously.

Hedging

The aim of hedging as outlined in the section 'Nature of futures trading' (i.e. pure hedging) is risk reduction. Risk avoidance in an *ex ante* sense is not possible, because as was seen in this section, hedging in a futures market, where the futures contracts are closed out by reversal, substitutes a basis risk for a price risk. Risk avoidance in an *ex post* sense may occur if spot and futures prices move in an exactly parallel fashion.

Pure hedging, then, is based on the assumption that risks are smaller with hedging than without. Using the variance of price as a measure of risk, we can write the risk per unit of unhedged stock as $V(S)$, and the risk per unit of hedged stock as

$$V(S) + V(F) - 2Cov_{SF},$$

which is likely to be less than $V(S)$, since normally one would expect movements of spot and futures prices to be closely correlated.[8]

The question of whether hedging reduces risks *ex post*, that is, whether profits and losses are smaller with hedging than without is considered in chapter 2.

Arbitrage

Arbitrage is a position taken in both spot and futures markets simultaneously, the aim of which is a certain profit.

The extent of this profit is normally known at the time the transaction is undertaken. For example, if the futures price exceeds the spot price by more than the cost of carrying the commodity until the maturity date of the future, a riskless profit can be made by buying spot, selling futures and making delivery under the futures contract. Similarly, if the spot price exceeds the futures price, it may be profitable for a stockholder who requires the commodity at a later date to sell the commodity spot, buy futures and take delivery under the futures contract (providing he can obtain delivery of a grade suitable for his requirements). In this way the user will avoid the carrying cost.

The first form of arbitrage aims to make a profit from contango, the second from backwardation. The two forms, however, are not symmetrical with respect to their effects on the price spread. They are further discussed in chapter 1.

Speculation

A speculator is one who, by virtue of his expectations and his willingness to take risk, aims to make an uncertain profit from his transactions in the market. This is so even though he holds his expectations with certainty (so called single-valued expectations), for there is no certainty that his expectations are correct.

A speculator may form his price expectations in terms of the futures price, the spot price, both spot and futures prices or in terms of the price spread alone. He may form his expectations in a precise manner, having in mind different expected prices for specific future dates with a definite idea of the likelihood that each will be achieved, or he may have only a vague notion that the price will change in a particular direction some time in the future.

A speculator may take a position in the spot market only, in the futures market only or in both spot and futures markets. A hedger who over- or under-hedges (or a stock-holder who carries his stock unhedged) is, of course, taking a speculative position with respect to the unhedged stock (or the futures contracts not covering a spot market commitment) for he is retaining a price risk and his expectation is one of uncertain profit.

A speculator may be risk-loving in the sense that he is willing to take a larger risk the larger his market position, or in the sense that he is willing to take a market position when he thinks the odds are against him, or he may be risk-averting in either or both of these senses.

Economists have used different behavioural assumptions to explain the market positions of speculators. They have sometimes assumed that speculators aim to maximize expected utility (see chapter 5), sometimes that they aim to maximize expected return subject to the constraint of risk minimization (see chapter 6), or that they aim to maximize expected net revenue (see chapter 4). In chapter 7 the author puts forward a theory where it is assumed that speculators adjust their market position so as to achieve a given risk of loss for any particular price expectation.

This book is based on a thesis accepted in partial fulfilment of the requirements for the degree of Doctor of Philosophy in Economics at the University of London (London School of Economics) in 1967.

Notes

1 B. S. Yamey, 'Short Hedging and Long Hedging in Futures Markets: Symmetry and Asymmetry', *Journal of Law and Economics*, October 1971.
2 Ibid.
3 See 'Categories of transaction' in this Introduction.
4 See Roger W. Gray, 'The Importance of Hedging in Futures Trading; and the Effectiveness of Futures Trading for Hedging', *Futures Trading Seminar*, vol. 1 (Madison, MIMIR, 1960).
5 See Yamey, op. cit.

6   H. S. Houthakker, 'The Scope and Limits of Futures Trading', *The Allocation of Economic Resources* (Stanford, 1959), p. 149.

7   Roger W. Gray, 'Why does Futures Trading Succeed or Fail: An Analysis of Selected Commodities', *Futures Trading Seminar*, vol. 3 (Wisconsin, MIMIR, 1966), pp. 115–28.

8   Let us assume here that the variances exist in an objective sense. This simplification is necessary because pure hedgers are usually assumed not to have any price expectations, or at least if they do, not to back them. Hence, the variances are not taken here to be the variances of subjective probability distributions of spot and futures prices.

The formula for the risk per unit of hedged stock is based on the notion that a hedge is a linear combination of spot and futures contracts. The formula is used by J. L. Stein and L. L. Johnson: see chapters 5 and 6.

I
The beginnings:
Keynes, Hicks and Kaldor

Keynes

In his *Treatise on Money* (London, 1930, vol. 2, p. 142) Keynes says that in an organized market for raw materials there are, at any one time, two price quotations. One is for immediate delivery (the spot price); the other is for delivery at a later date, say six months in the future (the forward price). For a producer whose period of production is six months, it is the latter price which is important in determining the extent of his operations. It may appear that it is the price which the producer expects in six months which is important in this respect, but Keynes's point is that he can sell the product forward even before the productive process is begun, and thereby hedge against the risk that the price will fall during the period of production.

This implies something about his attitude to risk; it assumes that he prefers certainty. Keynes goes on to say: 'If the futures price shows a profit on his cost of production he can go ahead and produce, selling his product forward, and running no risk.'

Keynes then examines three market situations. In the 'normal' case, where supply equals demand and no change in supply or demand conditions is expected, the spot price and the expected spot price coincide. Then the spot price

11

must exceed the forward price (backwardation) by the amount which the producer is willing to sacrifice to hedge himself against the risk of a price fall. That is, the spot price includes a risk premium, which the forward price does not (ibid., p. 143). So the normal case is one of backwardation, and the amount of the 'normal backwardation' is the hedger's marginal risk premium.

If there is a shortage of supply which can be remedied in six months, then the spot price may rise above the forward price to an extent which is limited by the willingness of the buyer to pay the higher spot price rather than postpone his purchases (ibid.). That is, there will be an abnormal backwardation. On this argument, if the shortage of supply could not be remedied in six months, one would expect the forward price to rise also, especially if the spot price was expected to keep on rising.

When there are surplus stocks, Keynes argues that a backwardation cannot exist (ibid., p. 144). For if there were a backwardation it would pay the stockholder to sell the stocks spot and buy them back forward, and so escape the carrying costs. The fact that he would wish to buy them back implies that his expected spot price exceeds both the spot and forward prices (or that he is committed to using the stocks at a later date); see p. 19.

So if surplus stocks exist F (the forward price) must exceed the spot price S (contango) and the contango must equal the storage, depreciation and interest charges of carrying the stocks. The reason for this is evidently that if the contango were less than this amount it would be profitable to sell the stocks spot and buy them back forward and so escape part of the carrying costs. Presumably this would continue until S had fallen to the required level. If the contango were greater than this amount it would pay to buy stocks spot and sell them forward and so make a riskless profit. This would continue until the contango was equal to the carrying costs (ibid.). So the equilibrium contango, as it were, according to Keynes, equals the carrying costs of the stock.

The terms 'surplus stocks' and 'shortage of supply' presumably indicate that the spot price is not in equilibrium, for if it were, the stocks would not be surplus (or short).

The existence of a contango, however, Keynes points out, does not mean that the producer can hedge without paying a risk premium as a price for certainty. In fact the price is likely to have risen because of the additional uncertainty due to the surplus stocks. That is, the forward price must be less than the expected spot price by at least the amount of the normal backwardation. This, however, seems to imply some uniformity in expectations.[1] For if the expected spot price of a particular trader were less than the forward price he would be paying a negative price for certainty.

So in Keynes's theory the hedger is a seller whose risk is that of a price fall. He makes his position certain by selling his product forward, and for the privilege of certainty he pays a particular price.

The hedger *qua* hedger, although he may have price expectations, does not act on them. Otherwise he would hedge when he expects the price to fall, and not when he expects it to rise. Therefore expectations do not enter into his hedging activities, although, as we have seen above, the use of price expectations is implied in some actions.

Suppose, however, that the hedger is a producer whose risk is that the price of inputs will rise. To avoid this risk he will make forward purchases of inputs. If he is to pay a premium for this certainty a contango will result, and the amount of the contango would under 'normal' conditions be equal to the marginal risk premium.

This assumes, however, that the risk is taken up by a speculator who carries no stocks of the commodity. The speculator then has to purchase and deliver the commodity at the forward date for which he would charge a premium. If the forward purchase is made from an individual who already possesses stocks, then the latter would also be entitled to recoup his carrying charges.

If hedger-sellers sold to hedger-buyers, then to the extent that one group pays a risk premium the other is being subsidized to accept certainty. So it is clear that Keynes's theory of normal backwardation assumes also that hedgers are predominantly sellers, and that the excess of selling hedges over buying hedges is taken up by speculators.

Hicks

Hicks, in his *Value and Capital* (London, 1953, pp. 135–40), views futures trading as a means of coordinating the plans of different groups, and so diminishing inconsistency of plans as a cause of disequilibrium between expected and actual prices.

He says that the 'ordinary businessman' only trades forward if he can make his position less risky by so doing; and that this is so only if he is already committed to make a purchase or sale in the future. Production rigidities, Hicks states, give less freedom in completing outputs than in buying inputs, once the production process has begun (ibid., p. 137).

One can think of many cases where rigidities give little freedom in purchase of inputs—for example, a builder who has contracted to finish a building by a particular date. And in this case these are the same rigidities which remove freedom in completing outputs. However, Hicks may have had his sausage-machine concept (*A Contribution to the Theory of the Trade Cycle*, London, 1956, p. 48) of the productive process in mind where output continues for a period even after raw material inputs have ceased. The critical point is that (apart from destroying the goods in process) one has no alternative but to complete the output. Production rigidities influence output in this example even after they have ceased to restrict freedom as regards inputs (except that the sausage-machine has to be kept going).

So if futures markets consisted only of hedgers, there would be an excess of hedged sales, and the forward price would be much below the expected spot price. This induces speculators to enter, purchase futures and expect a profit in so far as their expected spot price exceeds the forward price by at least the amount of their marginal risk premium. Their buying activity tends to raise the forward price (*Value and Capital*, p. 138).

This again assumes substantial uniformity of speculators' expectations. If there were a marked divergence of expectations this would result in transactions between speculators (see p. 17).

Hicks says that if the forward price is greater than the expected price minus the risk premium, the speculator leaves the market. There are, of course, other ways in which the individual can speculate—for example, he can buy spot if the spot price plus carrying costs and risk premium are less than his expected price. But Hicks seems to view the speculator as entering the market for the sole purpose of taking the excess of forward sales.

He misses an opportunity to develop the theory further by not considering what would happen to the forward price, and how backwardation would be interpreted, if there were an excess of long hedgers.

Hicks reaffirms Keynes's idea of normal backwardation as the price which hedgers pay to speculators (*Value and Capital*, p. 138) to avoid the risk of a price fall. He regards it as 'the cost of the co-ordination (of plans) achieved by forward trading' (ibid., pp. 138–9).

He also accords (ibid., p. 138n) with Keynes's position as regards contango which 'can only arise when spot prices are expected to rise sharply in the future; this usually means that spot prices are *abnormally* low' (italics in original). That is, the spot price is less than the forward price, which in turn is less than the expected spot price by at least the amount of the marginal risk premium. This corresponds to Keynes's case of the surplus stocks.

So Hicks, in taking over Keynes's theory, makes explicit or near explicit some of the implied assumptions, and states the model in a slightly more formal way. He did not, however, make any significant alteration to the theory. Neither did he make the assumptions as explicit as did some later writers (such as Kaldor, see pp. 16–26) and consequently he did not make clear the limited conditions under which the theory applies.

Kaldor

In Kaldor's model (*Essays on Economic Stability and Growth*, London, 1961, pp. 17–58) there are seven variables:

S	the spot price
F	the futures or forward price
E	expected spot price
i	marginal interest cost
c	marginal carrying cost (gross)
q	marginal convenience yield
$c-q$	is the marginal net carrying cost
r	marginal risk premium

The main variables are S, F and E. These three variables can be selected two at a time in $\dfrac{3!}{2!1!} = 3$ ways. There are, therefore, three main relationships:

1 between E and S
2 between S and F
3 between F and E

1 *Adjustment by speculators in spot of S with respect to E*
I shall deal with this adjustment for the case of multi-valued

expectations, where r is positive, and E means μ the mean of the individual's probability distribution of expected prices.

Speculation in spot, says Kaldor (ibid., p. 23), will result in an adjustment of S so that

$$E = S + i + (c - q) + r$$

This can be explained as follows:

The costs of buying and holding spot are $S + i + (c - q)$. If $E - r > S + i + (c - q)$, then speculators buy spot because they anticipate a return in excess of their marginal risk premium. Their demand price is therefore $E - \{i + (c - q) + r\}$. But if $E < S + i + (c - q) + r$, then no satisfactory return is expected, and speculators will sell spot.

Kaldor assumes that everyone has the same expectations in this part of the analysis (ibid., p. 28), but it is not necessary to assume this. Since S is the same for all individuals, it is necessary only that $E - i - (c - q) - r$ be the same for all. E, i, c, q and r can vary between individuals.

With heterogeneous expectations there will be transactions between speculators. If one is going to rule out such transactions, as Kaldor does in the early part of the analysis, then the adjustment does require uniform expectations. However, there seems to be no special advantage in ruling out transactions between speculators.

Kaldor calls this an adjustment of S. J. Dow ('Addenda to Mr Kaldor's Note', in 'A Symposium on the Theory of the Forward Market', *Review of Economic Studies*, vol. 7, June 1940, pp. 201–2), in pointing out that E, i, c, q and r may vary between individuals, describes this as an adjustment by individuals to the spot price. But it would seem that whether expectations are assumed uniform or not, there are really two adjustments:

   a individuals adjust to S, so that for each individual $E - \{i + (c - q) + r\} = S$. This may require some change in the *level* of i, c, q and r for the individual, given the functions of these variables in relation to stockholdings.

b when all individuals so adjust, there is likely to be some change in the level of S.

This raises the whole question of whether equilibrium is possible for an individual, and if so, whether it is stable. Kaldor assumes (op. cit., pp. 23, 24, 26) that

E is constant with respect to speculative stocks
r is an increasing function of such stocks (given the expectations distribution)
q is a diminishing function of speculative stocks
c is an increasing function of such stocks (for raw materials)
i is likely to be constant with respect to changes in speculative stocks.

The spot price S is fixed with respect to changes in the individual's stocks. This relationship is the supply curve of spot to the individual.

If $(c + r)$ is rising, or even falling, but less rapidly than q, then equilibrium is both possible and stable. $E - \{i + (c - q) + r\}$ becomes a diminishing function of speculative stocks. If, however, $(c + r)$ were to fall more rapidly than q, then equilibrium would be unstable. $E - \{i + (c - q) + r\}$ would be an increasing function of stocks.

Of course, if c, q and r were all constant, or if $(c + r)$ were to fall at the same rate as q, then equilibrium would be impossible, for then $E - \{i + (c - q) + r\}$ would have infinite elasticity.

J. Dow has criticized the relationship between E and S established by this adjustment on the grounds that it applies only to the case of 'positive' risks and does not apply when risks are 'negative'.

When stocks are held for sale at a later date, the stockholder has a positive risk (that the spot price will fall). This risk can be hedged by selling futures. But, says Dow, if the individual sells more futures than he has stocks, 'price changes will affect him the other way. This sort of risk may be called negative' (op. cit., p. 187). However, I suggest that this is not so. Although it is true that a fall in both prices may benefit him, his risk[2] is now that the futures price will rise, and this risk is positive, not negative.

2 Adjustment of F with respect to S

Arbitrage prevents F from exceeding S by more than the cost of arbitrage, which is $i + (c - q)$. For if F exceeds $S + i + (c - q)$, arbitrageurs can obtain a riskless profit by buying spot and selling forward. So arbitrage sets an upper limit to the contango (Kaldor, op. cit., pp. 24-5), and as a result

$$F \leqslant S + i + (c - q)$$

There is no limit, however, says Kaldor, to backwardation, apart from expectations. Keynes had attempted to establish a type of lower limit to F with respect to S when he argued that whenever $F < S + i + (c - q)$, it will be profitable for stockholders to sell their stocks spot and buy them back forward (see p. 12) and thereby avoid part of the carrying cost. This, of course, assumes either (i) that they have expectations which induce them to buy the stocks back; or (ii) that they are committed to use the stocks in a productive process at a later date.

This latter method of adjustment has been criticized by Gerda Blau ('Some Aspects of the Theory of Futures Trading', *Review of Economic Studies*, vol. 12, 1944-5, p. 11) on the grounds that it is limited by the quantity of stocks which arbitrageurs hold, and this quantity need not be sufficient to secure F equal to $S + i + (c - q)$. Thus, the two methods of arbitrage are not symmetrical.

Kaldor's method was to write:

$$E = S + i + (c - q) + r \qquad (1.1)$$
$$F = S + i + (c - q) \qquad (1.2)$$

By subtraction,

$$F = E - r \qquad (1.3)$$

So arbitrage prevents F from rising above $E - r$, while speculation prevents F from falling below $E - r$ because, if $F < E - r$, speculators will buy futures (Kaldor, op. cit., pp. 25–6).

This procedure does not appear to be logically satisfactory. Equation (1.2) has not been established. F has not been shown to be *equal* to $S + i + (c - q)$, but merely not to be greater than this amount. A preferable procedure would be to say

$$F \leqslant S + i + (c - q) \quad \text{by arbitrage}$$
$$F \geqslant E - r$$

because if $F < E - r$, speculators buy futures. This inequality should have been derived independently.

But

$$S + i + (c - q) = E - r \quad \text{from (1.1)}$$

Therefore

$$F = S + i + (c - q) \quad \text{which is (1.2)}$$
$$= E - r \quad \text{which is (1.3)}$$

3 *The third adjustment:* $F = E - r$
This results from arbitrage setting an upper limit to F with respect to S and speculation in futures setting a lower limit to F with respect to E. The two limits coincide as given by equation (1.1) so that F is uniquely determined at

$$S + i + (c - q) = E - r$$

The result, that $F = E - r$, is the main conclusion of Kaldor's model.[3]

20

I shall now rewrite the system in order to show that identical expectations are not required.

$$S = E - i - (c - q) - r$$
$$= J \text{ (say)} \tag{1.4}$$
$$F - S = i + (c - q)$$
$$= Q \text{ (say)} \tag{1.5}$$

Add:

$$F = J + Q$$
$$= E - r \tag{1.6}$$

Since S and F are the same for all individuals, it is necessary only that J and Q be the same for all.

However, the system does require that expectations are not too diverse. If an individual had a very low E he could not adjust to F; he would in effect be receiving a subsidy to sell futures and take risk. His marginal risk premium would be negative. This is contrary to Kaldor's intention, for he states that 'i and r are always positive' (ibid., p. 26).

Under what conditions is it true that $F = E - r$? In the *Essays*, Kaldor says that this conclusion is 'quite general' (ibid., p. 26) implying that it applies equally to situations where hedgers are predominantly sellers or predominantly buyers.

In an earlier article he had argued differently ('Speculation and Economic Stability', *Review of Economic Studies*, October 1939, pp. 1–27).

In situations where hedgers are buyers of futures, and speculators are spot buyers and forward sellers, he says that arbitrageurs (who are here included in 'speculators') do not get the convenience yield. The reason for this is that the convenience yield is 'the possibility of making use of them [the stocks] the moment they are wanted', and this is lost if the stocks are sold forward (ibid., p. 6).

The costs of arbitrage are therefore $i + c$, and not $i + (c - q)$ as before (ibid., p. 6). Although, as Kaldor points out, the carrying costs for ordinary holders are $(i + c - q)$ as before. Consequently a different result is reached. Equation (1.2) becomes $F = S + i + c$.

Then

$$E = S + i + (c - q) + r \qquad (1.7)$$
$$F = S + i + c \qquad (1.8)$$

By subtraction

$$F = E - r + q \qquad (1.9)$$

Whence F can exceed E in so far as q exceeds r.

J. Dow (op. cit., p. 186) had criticized this conclusion on the grounds that arbitrageurs do not lose the yield, because delivery is seldom made under a futures contract. Normally stock is hedged by sale of futures contracts, and when the stock is sold in the spot market, the futures contracts relating to it are closed out by buying an equivalent number of futures contracts. Dow points out that the result would have been different, of course, if the hedge had been made by selling the stock *forward*.

This, however, is no criticism of Kaldor's theory for it involves using a different concept of hedging. Kaldor is using the Keynes–Hicks concept of hedging where the stocks are sold forward and the forward contract is not re-purchased. It is clear that Kaldor is using this concept for, he says, 'By selling forward holders of stocks free themselves of any uncertainty' (op. cit., p. 5). With Dow's concept, however, hedging does not result in certainty, but merely replaces a basis risk for a price risk.

So it is no criticism of Kaldor's theory to say that arbitrageurs do not lose the yield when hedgers are buyers of futures, if this involves using a concept of hedging different from that which Kaldor is using.

In the *Essays*, however, Kaldor corrects this point, and argues that even when hedgers are buyers of futures, the costs of arbitrage are $i + (c - q)$, for whenever F exceeds

$S + i + (c - q)$ it will pay 'ordinary holders' to increase their stocks and sell futures at the same time (*Essays*, op. cit., p. 26, n. 1).

The result $F = E - r$ derived above seems to be an unhappy one where hedgers are net long in futures. In this case, speculators are net short. If $F = E - r$, they sell at the price F and expect to buy back at E, and hence expect to make a loss equivalent to the risk premium r.

Presumably the equilibrium condition for speculation in futures is

$$F = E + r \qquad (1.10)$$

The expected profit at the margin is the marginal risk premium.

Substituting from (1.10) into (1.1), for E, we get

$$F = S + i + (c - q) + 2r \qquad (1.11)$$

The result in (1.11), however, is not consistent with arbitrage by 'ordinary holders'.[4] Arbitrageurs will operate until the inequality $F \leqslant S + i + (c - q)$ is established.

The real difficulty seems to be the implicit assumption that long speculators in spot and short speculators in futures have the same expected spot price. If we drop this assumption and allow short speculators in futures to have the expected spot price E_F, then the equilibrium condition in (1.10) becomes

$$F = E_F + r \qquad (1.12)$$

Substituting from (1.12) into (1.2) for F, and adding r to both sides we have

$$E_F + 2r \leqslant S + i + (c - q) + r \qquad (1.13)$$

Substituting from (1.1) into the right-hand side of (1.13) we get the result

$$E_F + 2r \leqslant E \qquad (1.14)$$

That is, short speculators in futures have an expected spot

23

price less than the expectation of speculators in spot, by an amount which is at least equal to twice the marginal risk premium. This result seems more reasonable, since it is presumably their lower expected price which leads speculators in futures to be on the short side of the market.[5]

Kaldor then shows that the conclusion $F = E - r$ is consistent with various market situations.

1 When speculative stocks are zero, $E = S$

Then

$$i + (c - q) + r = 0 \quad \text{from (1.1)}$$

therefore

$$i + r = -(c - q)$$

But i and r are always positive, so that the net carrying cost $(c - q)$ must be negative. Therefore q must exceed c. Since $E = S$

$$F = S - r \quad \text{from (1.3)}$$

That is, F is less than S by the amount of Keynes's normal backwardation (*Essays*, p. 26).

However, it seems to follow from equation (1.1) that it is not necessary to have E equal to S for speculative stocks to be zero. If E exceeds S by an amount insufficient to cover $i + (c - q) + r$, then spot speculators will sell their stocks until speculative stocks are zero (and this may occur while E still exceeds S) or until (1.1) is achieved.

Since $F = E - r$, it is possible that F could exceed S. So contango is compatible with zero speculative stocks in Kaldor's model.

2 When stocks are scarce

q is large and is likely to exceed $i + c + r$, and S will exceed E—that is, a fall in the spot price is expected.

But F is less than E by an amount r, so that S exceeds F by more than r. There is, therefore, abnormal backwardation (ibid.). The amount of the abnormal backwardation is the excess of q over $i + c$, that is

$$S - F = q - (i + c) \quad \text{from (1.2)}$$

Gerda Blau, however, argues that the marginal convenience yield is never large. She says that q relates to stocks outside 'immediate requirements' (op. cit., p. 6). But Kaldor's convenience yield does not apply only to stocks outside immediate requirements.

Miss Blau is talking about working capital. Of this Kaldor says (*Essays*, p. 26):

a Speculative stocks means excess of stocks over 'requirements'
b Marginal convenience yield falls sharply with an increase in stocks above 'requirements'
c Carrying costs are likely to be positive when speculative stocks are positive, and negative when speculative stocks are negative.

So it is clear that Kaldor means his convenience yield to refer to stocks which are part of 'requirements'. Miss Blau's point is therefore no refutation of Kaldor's argument.

It is true, however, that a backwardation requires a substantial positive q. This is quite a burden to lay at the door of the convenience yield, especially as Kaldor argues that there is no limit, apart from expectations, to backwardation.

Diverse expectations
After having unnecessarily assumed identical expectations in the initial model, Kaldor then goes on to deal explicitly with the case of diverse expectations. He seems to agree that identical expectations are not essential to the first model for he says, in the *Symposium* (p. 201), that the Hicks–Keynes

doctrine that $F = E - r$ is not true if 'there is a marked divergence in individual expectations'.

Kaldor deals with the case of diverse expectations in an intuitive, rather than an analytical way.

He divides speculators into two groups: bulls, who expect the spot price to rise, and bears, who expect it to fall. Bulls will therefore buy futures with a demand price for each individual of $E - r$, where E is the mean of the individual's distribution of expected prices, and r is his marginal risk premium (*Essays*, p. 28). Bears will sell futures and the supply price of each individual seller will be $E + r$.

If by E, says Kaldor, one means an average expectation for all speculators (I shall call it $\bar{E}$), then the forward price will be established in the range $\bar{E} \pm r$. The opposite risks assumed by bulls and bears tend to cancel out leaving F close to $\bar{E}$. A predominance of bulls tends to raise F above $\bar{E}$; a predominance of bears tends to depress F below $\bar{E}$. Selling hedgers strengthen bearish forces while buying hedgers support bullish forces (ibid., p. 29).

Unfortunately most of the precision of the early model has been lost here. The meaning of the range $\bar{E} \pm r$ is not clear, for no precise meaning has been given to r.[6] Nor is Kaldor's general conclusion much help. He says that where there is marked divergence of opinion the futures price 'will reflect the "expected" price' (ibid.).

Kaldor does not discuss the adjustment of the spot price in relation to the expected price, where expectations are diverse. There is only a passing reference to S: that F cannot exceed S by more than the cost of arbitrage (*Essays*, p. 29).

Notes

1 Kaldor's 'not much divergence of expectations' condition; see pp. 25–6. This implication appears to be true also of the 'normal' situation and when supplies are short.

2 That is, in relation to the excess sales of futures. For a possible risk in relation to hedged stock, see chapter 2.

3 It may appear that Kaldor's system is over-determined, for he says on p. 27 that if $F > E - r$, hedgers will sell futures. If this statement were taken at face value it would be both unnecessary and unfortunate, for it would imply that hedgers form expectations and act upon them. I suggest, however, that this statement can be reconciled with Kaldor's theory if it is taken to mean that if $F > S + i + (c - q)$, then hedgers, being 'ordinary holders' and acting as arbitrageurs, will buy spot and sell futures; and of course, given equilibrium in the spot market, $S + i + (c - q) = E - r$, from equation (1.1).

4 The presence of 'ordinary holders', who may be short hedgers, is compatible with the model, so long as the assumption that long hedgers predominate is not violated.

5 Suppose that the expectations of speculators in futures are correct, so that the realized spot price at the end of the period S_1, is equal to E_F. Then

$$F = S_1 + r \quad \text{from (1.12)}$$

That is, hedgers make a loss equal to the marginal risk premium. (Speculators in futures make a profit equal to this amount.)

On the other hand, if the expectations of speculators in spot are correct, i.e. $E = S_1$, then

$$F + r \leqslant S_1$$

or

$$S_1 - F \geqslant r$$

from (1.12) and (1.14).

That is, hedgers make a profit at least equal to the marginal risk premium. (Speculators in futures make a loss at least equal to this amount.)

6 Perhaps r could be defined as $\bar{r}$: an average marginal risk premium for all individuals. But it is not clear that this adds anything to the result. One could assume that marginal risk premiums are identical, but this, as Kaldor says, seems unsatisfactory when expectations are assumed diverse.

2

The concept of hedging

The 'old' concept of hedging

The concept of hedging used in the literature, changed between 1940 and 1950. Keynes (op. cit.), Hicks (op. cit.), Kaldor (in the *Essays*) and Blau (op. cit.) use the 'old' concept, while Working ('Futures Trading and Hedging', *American Economic Review*, June 1953, vol. 43, pp. 314–43) and some later writers use a different concept, which is, however, evident to some extent in Dow (op. cit., see p. 22 above).

The characteristics of the early concept of hedging are as follows. First, hedging made the hedger's position certain. He sold his product forward and made delivery under the contract and, in fact, his aim in hedging was certainty.

Keynes is explicit that hedging eliminates risk. He says: 'If this [futures] price shows a profit on his costs of production, then he can go full steam ahead, selling his product forward and *running no risk*.' (Op. cit., p. 142, italics mine.) Again: 'If supply and demand are balanced, the spot price must exceed the forward price by the amount which the producer is ready to sacrifice in order to "hedge" himself, i.e. *to avoid the risk of price fluctuations during his production period*.' (Op. cit., p. 143, italics mine.)

Hicks, although taking over Keynes's theory and concepts, speaks of the risk of a price change being reduced rather than 'avoided'. He says 'the ordinary businessman only enters into a forward contract if by so doing he can "hedge"—that is to say, if the forward transaction lessens the riskiness of his position' (op. cit., p. 137). Later we read: '. . . if these planned supplies can be covered by forward sales, risk is reduced' (ibid.). It may be that the term 'is reduced' applies to the seller's overall position, for it is clear that in the latter case the risk of a fall in the spot price is eliminated.

In the *Essays* (p. 24) Kaldor describes 'hedgers' as 'those who have certain commitments independent of any transactions in the forward market, . . . and who enter the forward market in order to reduce the risks arising out of these commitments'. He thus speaks of hedging as 'reducing' rather than 'eliminating' risks.

It is clear, however, that he views hedging as achieving a complete reduction of risk, because in the original article ('Speculation and Economic Stability', p. 5) he says: 'By selling forward holders of stocks free themselves of any uncertainty.'

Gerda Blau takes a similar position when she says that 'his [the hedger's] motive is not profit but security' (op. cit., p. 13). However, she does not state explicitly whether hedging results in certainty.

The second characteristic of the early concept of hedging is that a hedger does not act on his expectations; he was usually assumed not to have any expectations. If he were a seller-hedger (the most usual case) he always sold forward irrespective of any expectations about the future spot price.

Keynes, Hicks and Kaldor do not say explicitly that hedgers have no expectations, but they do not give the expected price any role in the hedger's actions. Later writers, however, have made definite statements on this point. Hawtrey ('Mr Kaldor on the Forward Market', *Review of Economic Studies*, June 1940, p. 203) says: 'But even if hedgers are to be regarded as potential speculators, that does not mean that they regularly form expectations of price movements', and very clearly that 'he [the hedger] may quite possibly form an opinion, but he does not back it' (ibid.).

Miss Blau takes a similar position. She says 'a trader's decision to hedge will be influenced by past experiences concerning the degree of price-variability in the market in general—rather than by any very definite expectations concerning price developments' (op. cit., p. 13). Later she argues that: 'The hedger has no "expected price" because he does not want to base his calculations on his opinions concerning the spot price at the forward date' (ibid., p. 14).

Third, with the earlier concept, a hedger was always a pure hedger; that is, he carried a full hedge. For example, if he were a seller-hedger he would sell futures corresponding to the amount of stock he carried, neither more nor less. To the extent that he failed to do this he was speculating. Thus Kaldor says: 'Ordinary stockholders and producers of the commodity may of course also indulge in speculation, in so far as they carry extra stocks in the expectation of a rise in price' (*Essays*, p. 241).

The last two characteristics, disregard of expectations and full hedging, follow from the first. If the hedger's aim is certainty, and since hedging results in certainty, then he should always hedge his stocks irrespective of his expectations, for otherwise he is not divorcing himself from the risk of a price change. Similarly, if he fails to carry a full hedge, he cannot achieve certainty.

The later concept of hedging

With the later concept of hedging, the procedure and characteristics are different. The risk of a stockholder who has just bought stocks in the spot market is that the spot price will fall. He can hedge against this risk by selling futures

31

contracts. At a later date he will sell the stock in the spot market, and close out his futures market commitments by buying a quantity of the particular futures contracts equal to the number he had originally sold.[1]

It is clear that hedging in this way does not make the hedger's position certain; it substitutes a basis risk for a price risk (the 'basis' is the difference between spot and futures prices at a given point of time, i.e. $S_t - F_t$). If the spot price rises more quickly or falls less rapidly than the forward price during the period for which the hedge is carried—that is, if the basis increases—then a seller-hedger will make a profit. Conversely, a decline in the basis will yield a loss, while if S and F move at the same rate and in the same direction—that is, if the basis is constant—he will make neither a profit nor a loss.

The question is then whether hedging reduces risks *ex post*—that is, whether hedging reduces the effect, upon the hedger, of fluctuations in the spot price. B. S. Yamey has investigated this problem ('An Investigation of Hedging on an Organised Produce Exchange', *Manchester School*, September 1951, pp. 305–19) by obtaining the results for samples of hypothetical hedges in cotton futures on the Liverpool Cotton Exchange for the period 1930–40.

He classified his results according to whether hedges were:

> *a* Perfect (i.e. no gain or loss in hedged position)
>
> *b* Over-compensating (i.e. spot market losses became gains in the hedged position)
>
> *c* Under-compensating (i.e. spot market losses reduced)
>
> *d* Aggravating (i.e. spot market losses increased by hedging)

He always assumed that the hedger was on the losing side of the change in the spot price—that is, long in spot for a fall in the spot price, and short in spot for a rise (ibid., pp. 307, 314).

His conclusion was that overall, gains and losses are smaller with hedging than without (ibid., p. 319), although 'aggravating' hedges occurred in 7 per cent of the sample results. Such 'aggravating' hedges, however, occurred only when spot price changes were small (ibid., p. 313). Groups (*a*), (*b*) and (*c*) comprised 4 per cent, 41 per cent and 48 per cent respectively of the sample results (ibid., p. 313).

Truman F. Graf's investigation produced somewhat similar results ('Hedging—How Effective is it?', *Journal of Farm Economics*, August 1953, pp. 398–413). He studied the wheat, corn and oats markets at the Chicago Board of Trade for the period 1949–51. He measured the effectiveness of hedging by the percentage decrease in gain or loss of the spot transaction due to hedging, for a series of hypothetical short hedges.

The average effectiveness of hedging for the three-year period for each grain was: wheat 35·53 per cent, corn 26·68 per cent and oats 41·00 per cent. For all three grains the average effectiveness was approximately 35 per cent (ibid., pp. 402, 411).

When the three years were each divided into four seasons, hedges were found to be ineffective (i.e. effectiveness < 0): for wheat, one season in twelve; corn, one season in twelve; and oats, two seasons in twelve. Of 149 hedges in each commodity, 108 were found to be effective in wheat, 99 in corn and 109 in oats (ibid., pp. 402, 404).

Graf also found that hedges tended to be more effective in periods when spot price changes were large (ibid., p. 407).

This leads to the question of what is the aim of the hedger in futures market dealings? Yamey says that if the hedge results in neither a profit nor a loss the hedge is 'perfect' (op. cit., p. 307). This implies that the aim of the hedger is risk reduction, and indeed, he says later that 'hedging is based on the assumption that S and F are likely to move in correspondence' (ibid., p. 307). Moreover, one of the conclusions of the study is: 'If this [that hedging results in smaller gains and losses] were generally true, it would provide strong justification for the practice of hedging to reduce the risk of price fluctuation' (ibid., p. 307).

This is not so for H. Working, however, who argues that hedging is usually done in conjunction with the expectation of a favourable change in the basis. He makes it clear that hedging in his sense contains a speculative element when he says: 'Such discretionary hedging involving a firm in the practice of both hedging and speculation, . . . seems to be especially prevalent among dealers and processors who handle commodities such as wool and coffee' (op. cit., p. 320), and later that: 'It is mainly a form of arbitrage, undertaken most commonly in expectation of a favourable change in the relation between spot and futures prices' (ibid., p. 342). He later redefined hedging to be the temporary substitution of a futures contract for a merchandising contract ('Hedging Reconsidered', *Journal of Farm Economics*, November 1953, p. 560; and 'New Concepts Concerning Futures Markets and Prices', *American Economic Review*, vol. 52, 1962, p. 432).

This represents a loss in precision compared with the earlier terminology. The term 'hedging' no longer enables one to distinguish between risk avoidance, arbitrage and speculation. This loss, I suggest, is unnecessary. While the act of selling futures gives no outward indication of whether the aim is risk avoidance, a certain profit, or uncertain profit, it is still possible to distinguish these transactions *conceptually*, and for the purposes of economic theory it seems desirable to do so.

The association in the literature of hedging with the motive of an uncertain profit is a reasonable consequence of the fact that hedging does not result in certainty. If hedging leaves a risk then expectations become relevant; and if a loss from hedging is expected it would be unwise to hedge. On the other hand, if a profit is expected it would appear advantageous to hedge.

The third characteristic of the new concept of hedging, which is a logical consequence of the association of hedging with the aim of an uncertain profit, is that a hedger may no longer carry a full hedge: he may sell more or less futures than he has spot. For example, if a stockholder expects the spot price to rise faster than the futures price, he may back his expectations by carrying part of his stock unhedged.

For the purpose of continuity and precision I shall, in what follows, use the terms 'hedging', 'arbitrage' and 'speculation' in their earlier senses. That is, I shall take 'hedging' to mean a transaction in the futures market for the purpose of avoidance or reduction of a spot market price risk. By 'arbitrage' I shall mean simultaneous dealing in spot and futures with the aim of a riskless profit. While 'speculation' will be interpreted as entering either market with a view to profit, where such market commitments involve taking on a new risk.

Note

1   He will do this only if it is more profitable than making delivery under the futures contract.

Profit for delivery under the futures contract is $F_1 - S_1$ (ignoring costs of carrying the stock—subscripts refer to the time period). The profit from reversing the futures contracts and selling in the spot market is:

$$(S_2 - S_1) - (F_2 - F_1) = (S_2 - F_2) - (S_1 - F_1)$$

where $(S_2 - S_1)$ is profit on spot and $(F_2 - F_1)$ is loss on futures contracts.

The stockholder will sell in the spot market if

$$(S_2 - F_2) - (S_1 - F_1) > F_1 - S_1$$

That is, if

$$(S_2 - F_2) > 0$$

It is clear that if the futures contract is held to maturity, so that $S_2 = F_2$ (where F_2 refers to the price, at $t = 2$, of the particular future initially sold, which is not necessarily the same as the price of a new future at $t = 2$), then the later concept of hedging also results in certainty, and the short hedger is indifferent between reversal of the futures contract, and delivery under that contract.

Thus the 'old' concept of hedging may be viewed as a special case of the later concept, where a full hedge is carried and all futures contracts are held to maturity.

If account is taken of carrying costs, when delivery is made under the futures contract, the profit is equal to $F_1 - \{S_1 + i + (c - q)\}$.

Where the futures contracts are reversed and the stock is sold spot, the profit is

$$[S_2 - \{S_1 + i + (c - q)\}] - (F_2 - F_1) =$$
$$(S_2 - F_2) - [\{S_1 + i + (c - q)\} - F_1]$$

using Kaldor's notation.

The stockholder will therefore sell in the spot market if

$$(S_2 - F_2) - [\{S_1 + i + (c - q)\} - F_1] >$$
$$F_1 - \{S_1 + i + (c - q)\}$$

that is

$$(S_2 - F_2) > 0$$

3
Theories of market equilibrium: Peston and Yamey

Three theories of market equilibrium will be dealt with in chapters 3 and 4: those of Peston and Yamey, Brennan and Telser. The first of these will be discussed in this chapter and the last two in the following chapter. In part, the theories of Brennan and Telser treat the question of market equilibrium in a similar way, and to this extent they are given a common discussion.

In the basic Peston and Yamey model ('Inter-Temporal Price Relationships with Forward Markets: a Method of Analysis', *Economica*, November 1960, pp. 355–67), the main problem is to allocate a fixed stock of a commodity between consumption in the current period and storage, and to determine the spot and forward prices.

Traditional demand and supply analysis is used— 'traditional' in the sense that demand and supply curves for the several markets are derived, and an equilibrium price is determined by their intersection. The question is then whether this equilibrium is stable.

The assumptions are: first, that the markets formed by the various groups of operators are perfectly competitive. Second, expectations about the spot price for future periods are assumed given (ibid., p. 355); but they are not assumed homogeneous, nor is any particular assumption made about their nature (single or multivalued, symmetrically or asymmetrically distributed).

Three groups of operators are assumed (ibid., pp. 355–6):

a Hedgers, who carry stocks and divorce their risks by selling futures equal to the quantity of stocks they intend to carry over to the next period. Their actions are determined on the basis of *S* and *F*: they have no expectations.

This group consists of hedgers in the 'old' sense; there is no indication that the futures contracts are bought back, and '*ex definitione* the hedger is not subject to market risk' (ibid., p. 357).

b Merchants, who carry unhedged stocks, and determine their actions on the basis of the current spot price and their expectations about the future spot price. Merchants are really speculators in spot.

c Speculators, who buy futures contracts according to the level of the futures price relative to their expectations about the future spot price.

Three markets are distinguished:

1 The *market for storage*, in which *demand* comes from those who plan to be holders of stocks in the next period, that is, from:

a Merchants who hold unhedged stocks
b Speculators, because of their holdings of futures contracts

It would seem that speculators plan to be momentary holders only and intend to sell their stocks spot upon delivery, as they are assumed to carry no stocks.

The *supply* of storage is provided by those who hold stocks during the current period, that is, by:

a Hedgers who hold hedged stocks; and
b Merchants who hold unhedged stocks. That is, the

38

carrying of unhedged stocks by merchants from the current period to the next involves a reciprocal supply and demand for storage on their part.

2   In the *market for futures* the *supply* of futures contracts is provided by hedgers, and the *demand* comes from speculators in futures.

3   There is also a *market for present consumption*—a spot market—in which *demand* is assumed given, and independent of the demand and supply conditions in the other two markets. Consumers are assumed not to carry stocks, and the whole of the stock to be allocated is carried by hedgers and merchants.

Supply in the spot market is that part of the stock which is not allocated to storage.

For hedgers there are two alternatives: to sell now or to sell futures and carry the stock over. Stockholding becomes more attractive the larger the contango, so that the supply of hedged storage is an increasing function of $F - S$. Therefore, given S, the supply of storage by hedgers is an increasing function of F.

This relationship is drawn as a linear curve with a positive gradient. The positive slope is said to derive from the marginal net carrying cost of stock which, following Kaldor, is defined as the marginal carrying cost less the marginal convenience yield. Marginal carrying costs are assumed to be a direct function of the level of stocks and the marginal convenience yield is assumed to be an inverse function of this quantity, so that marginal net carrying cost varies directly with the volume of stocks carried (ibid., p. 357, n. 1; see also chapter 1 above). Using Kaldor's notation, if $F > S + i + (c - q)$, then the stocks will be carried over until $F = S + i + (c - q)$ or until all stocks are sold forward, whichever is the sooner. Similarly, if $F < S + i + (c - q)$, then the stocks will be sold spot until

39

$F = S + i + (c - q)$ or until all stocks are sold spot, whichever is the sooner.

The supply of storage by hedgers does, of course, vary inversely with the spot price, given F.

Merchants carry stocks because a rise in the spot price is expected,[1] and determine their actions according to their expectations, and the current spot price. Demand for (and supply of) storage by merchants has zero elasticity with respect to F.

Given the individual merchants' expectations, the higher S the more costly it is to hold stocks (in terms of opportunity cost). That is, demand for (and hence supply of) storage by merchants is a diminishing function of S, say Peston and Yamey (op. cit.).[2]

However, the demand for (and supply of) storage is drawn as a functional relationship between the quantity of storage and the forward price, for a given spot price.

For speculators, who are buyers of futures, the holding of futures contracts becomes more attractive the lower F, given their expectations. Therefore the demand for futures by speculators (W) is a diminishing function of F (ibid.). It is not affected by changes in the spot price.

Consumption demand U is a decreasing function of the spot price; it is not affected by changes in the forward price.

There are three equilibrium conditions:

> The total stock must be allocated between storage and present consumption.
> The spot price and the forward price must equate demand and supply in the consumption and futures markets respectively.

Only two of these conditions, however, are independent. For example, if the quantity of storage and forward price are in equilibrium, then the quantity of present consumption and the spot price must also be in equilibrium (ibid., p. 358, n. 2).

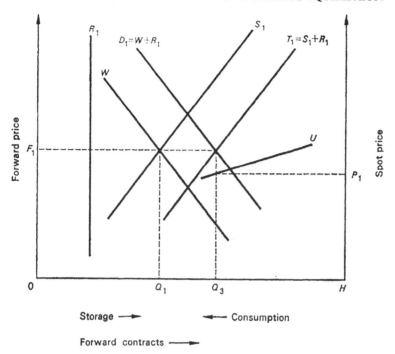

Figure 1 *Determination of spot and futures prices*
(from Peston and Yamey, 1960)

The model is presented diagrammatically as follows:

S_1 is the supply of hedged stocks by hedgers. It is drawn for a given spot price, say P_1. For a higher spot price it would shift to the left

R_1 is the supply of (and demand for) unhedged storage by merchants. It is drawn for a given spot price P_1. With a higher spot price it would shift to the left

W is the demand for futures contracts (and consequently for storage) by speculators

U is the demand for present consumption

These are the four basic functional relationships. Other functions are:

41

D, the total demand for storage by speculators and merchants, which is the horizontal sum of the W and R_1 curves at each forward price

T, the total supply of storage by hedgers and merchants, which is the horizontal sum of the R_1 and S_1 curves (ibid., p. 359).

The total stock of the commodity to be allocated is $0H$. The quantities of storage and of forward contracts are measured from left to right on the horizontal axis, and consumption is measured in the opposite direction. The forward price is shown on the left-hand ordinate, while the spot price is shown on the right.

The equilibrium forward price F_1 is determined by the intersection of the W and S_1 curves (or alternatively of the D_1 and T_1 curves). The total quantity of storage forthcoming at this price is $0Q_3$, of which $0Q_1$ is supplied by hedgers (which is also the quantity of futures contracts supplied by them), and Q_1Q_3 is supplied by merchants.

This leaves HQ_3 for present consumption, which, given the demand for consumption U, is sold at spot price P_1. Thus, Peston and Yamey say: 'It will be seen that the two markets are in equilibrium with present price P_1, and price of forward contracts $p_1 (= F_1)$' (op. cit., p. 359).

I suggest that this equilibrium can be explained as follows. (It is not, I believe, fully explained in the original article.) There exist an infinite number of pairs of D and T curves, each uniquely tied to a particular spot price P. The problem is to determine the equilibrium trilogy. The resulting trilogy must yield a forward price F (and therefore a quantity of storage $0Q$), which leaves a quantity of current consumption QH such that the latter is cleared from the market at the spot price in the trilogy. Only one spot price will do this.

The assumption of a fixed stock is seen to be critical. If the stock were not fixed, any set of D, T and P would suffice; the forward price and quantity of storage would then be determined, and the quantity of current consumption (and production) would adjust to the spot price.

This equilibrium is also seen to be stable. For suppose the spot price were to rise above P_1: this would give rise to excess supply in the spot market. In addition the R_1 and S_1 functions would shift to the left, so that the quantities of unhedged storage and of hedged storage would decline, and the forward price would rise. There would then be further excess supply in the spot market, which would lead to a reduction in the spot price to P_1' (ibid., p. 360).

This is a Keynes-type model in two respects. First, the 'old' concept of hedging is used: the hedger is not subject to market risk (ibid., p. 357), does not back his expectations and always carries a full hedge. Second, the forward price is determined solely by the actions of seller-hedgers and buyer-speculators. Storage demanded and supplied by merchants has no influence on the forward price, because this quantity is added equally to the total demand for, and total supply of, storage.

On the other hand, it is not a Keynes-type model in that there is no precise relationship between the forward price and the expected price. In fact, there is no one expected price. Expectations do influence the forward price however, because they are a parameter of the demand for forward contracts, W.

Of course 'the' expected price (the mean of the individual's distribution of expected prices) must exceed the forward price for some speculators, for otherwise no futures contracts would be demanded.

The model does not specify any equilibrium relationship between the forward price and the spot price. Unhedged storage will be supplied whether there is contango or backwardation, being insensitive to the forward price. For hedged storage to be forthcoming, the condition is that

$$F \geqslant S + i + (c - q)$$

43

Some hedged storage may be supplied when there is back-wardation if the marginal convenience yield is large enough (ibid., p. 357, n. 1).[3]

It would appear, however, that the model cannot be in full equilibrium if the forward price exceeds $S + i + (c - q)$, for then seller-hedgers would be induced to act as arbitrageurs, buying stocks spot and selling them forward, thus earning a riskless profit. Arbitrage therefore results in the equilibrium condition $F \leqslant S + i + (c - q)$.

This, together with the condition for the provision of hedged storage, seems to lead to the conclusion that this model is in full equilibrium only if the additional condition $F = S + i + (c - q)$ is also met. Furthermore, it would appear that this equality will be achieved, as a result of the actions of the 'hedgers' group (acting as both hedgers and arbitrageurs).

Notes

1 Or for trading reasons say Peston and Yamey (op. cit., p. 358) (i.e. to derive the convenience yield), but this amounts to the same thing (unless the convenience yield is very high).

2 This inverse relationship would appear to derive from the assumption that the marginal net carrying cost $i + (c - q)$ is an increasing function of stocks held. The merchant's diminishing stockholding schedule could then be explained by equating at the margin $E - i - (c - q)$ and the spot price. If the marginal net carrying cost were constant, it would appear to be most profitable for the merchant to hold his maximum quantity of stocks for all values of S less than $E - i - (c - q)$; that is, demand for (and supply of) storage by the individual merchant would have zero elasticity with respect to S. Demand for (and supply of) storage by merchants as a group would be a diminishing function of S only if individual expectations and/or marginal net carrying costs were heterogeneous. (Marginal risk premiums are ignored here, since no particular assumptions are made about the nature of expectations.)

3 Since my purpose is to discuss the basic Peston and Yamey

model only, I have not considered the modifications made to this model by the introduction of 'mixed traders' (hedger-merchants) and 'mixed speculators' (speculators who buy both spot and futures). The reader who is interested in this question should refer to the original article.

4
Theories of market equilibrium: Brennan and Telser

The purpose of this chapter is to discuss the general storage models of Brennan ('The Supply of Storage', *American Economic Review*, March 1958, pp. 50–72) and Telser ('Futures Trading and the Storage of Cotton and Wheat', *Journal of Political Economy*, June 1958, pp. 233–55), which are developed in the absence of futures trading.

In Brennan's model, a two-period model, there are two categories of operator: consumers, and 'merchants', who are really speculators in spot.

The demand for storage comes from consumers. This differs from the Peston and Yamey treatment where the demand for unhedged storage is provided by 'merchants', whose expectations involve them in a reciprocal demand for and supply of storage. Brennan's treatment, although it removes the distinction between the storage and consumption markets, is appropriate in the context of this question. If he were to treat merchants as both demanders and suppliers of storage there would be one category of operator only. There would then be no market equilibrium, but only an 'internal' equilibrium for merchants.

Brennan's demand for storage function is derived as follows: since there is assumed to be an inverse relationship between consumption in any period t, C_t, and price in that period P_t,

$$P_t = f_t(C_t) \qquad (4.1)$$

where

$$\frac{\partial P_t}{\partial C_t} < 0$$

Also $C_t = S_{t-1} + X_t - S_t$ where X_t is production in period t, and S_t is closing stock of period t.
Hence

$$P_t = f_t(S_{t-1} + X_t - S_t) \qquad (4.2)$$

Now $\partial C_t / \partial S_t < 0$, so that $\partial P_t / \partial S_t > 0$.
And $\partial C_{t+1} / \partial S_t > 0$, so that $\partial P_{t+1} / \partial S_t < 0$.
Hence the demand for storage function is written as

$$P_{t+1} - P_t = f_{t+1}(S_t + X_{t+1} - S_{t+1}) - \\ f_t(S_{t-1} + X_t - S_t) \qquad (4.3)$$

where $\partial(P_{t+1} - P_t)/\partial S_t < 0$, and S_{t-1}, X_t, S_{t+1} and X_{t+1} are taken as given.

The demand for storage function, therefore, gives the actual price change as a function of the closing stock of the first period, *ceteris paribus*.

The suppliers of storage, merchants, are assumed to exist in a competitive market, to hold their expectations with uncertainty and to have the aim of maximization of expected net revenue $E(NR)$ (that is, expected revenue less net storage costs).

For $E(NR)$ to be a maximum

$$\begin{aligned} m_t &= E(MR) \\ &= E(P_{t+1} - P_t) \quad \text{under competition} \\ &= E(P_{t+1}) - P_t \end{aligned} \qquad (4.4)$$

where the marginal net cost of storage

$$m_t' = o_t + r_t' - c_t',$$

and

$$\begin{aligned} \sigma^t &= \text{marginal cost of storage proper} \\ r_t' &= \text{marginal risk aversion factor} \\ c_t' &= \text{marginal convenience yield} \\ E(MR) &= \text{expected marginal revenue[1]} \end{aligned}$$

Equation (4.4) is the same as Kaldor's equilibrium condition for speculation in spot (*Essays*, p. 23).

The individual firm's supply of storage function is therefore an increasing function of the closing stocks of period t, S_t.

On the assumptions of competition and no external economies or diseconomies of storage, the industry supply of storage function $g_t(S_t)$ is the sum of the individual firms' supply functions.

This treatment does not imply identical expectations although this is the assumption which Brennan makes (op. cit., p. 56).

Equilibrium in this storage market requires that the quantity of storage be such that actual and expected price changes are equal. This will occur when the demand for storage, which is a consumption demand, equals the supply of storage, which is a speculative supply. Stockholders will then be under no inducement to change their quantities of storage, because they will be maximizing expected net revenue, and their expectations will be correct.

This equilibrium condition is written as:

$$g_t(S_t) = f_{t+1}(S_t + X_{t+1} - S_{t+1}) - \\ f_t(S_{t-1} + X_t - S_t) \qquad (4.5)$$

The model is in equilibrium when the price change is $0R$, and the quantity of stocks carried out of period t is $0L$ (see Figure 2).

There appear to be two main difficulties with this model. One is that the model contains no mechanism to bring equilibrium about. If expectations are identical and the mean expectation is $0R$, then equilibrium will be instantaneously achieved.

If, however, the mean expectation is $0S$, then the quantity of storage will be $0M$, the actual price change $0T$, and firms will take an unexpected profit. Firms may revise their

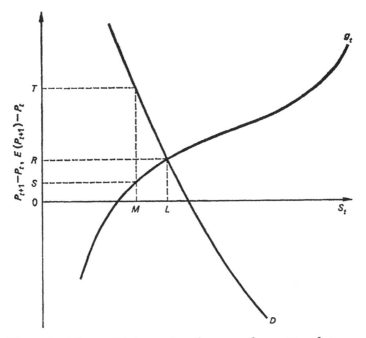

Figure 2   The equilibrium price change and quantity of storage
(from M. J. Brennan, 1958)

expectations and hence their supply of storage, but there is nothing to force them to do so. As long as the number of suppliers is constant, firms may go on taking these un-expected profits, and the so-called 'disequilibrium' price change will continue.

Apparently to cope with these difficulties, Telser has argued (op. cit., pp. 237–8) that if expectations are con-sistently wrong, then firms suffer losses and some are forced to leave the group, or else they make profits and new firms enter. Stability of the number of firms in the group (the cotton and wheat markets studied by Telser) leads to the presumption that firms' expectations are correct on average.

This, however, seems to be an unsatisfactory explanation. First, it is not an analytical demonstration of how equilib-rium is achieved, but rather an assertion that equilibrium exists. Second, the equilibrium indicated by stability of the number of firms is long-run, whereas the model appears to require a short-run equilibrium. (See, for example, Kaldor's statement that 'speculation is essentially a short period commitment'. [*Essays*, p. 23.]) Are we to take Telser's argument to mean that no short-run equilibrium is possible? Clearly, it is possible that profits may balance losses, so that the number of firms is stable, yet the system may be in continuous short-run disequilibrium.[2]

Brennan, in his estimation of the supply of storage function, uses an expectations hypothesis in which the adjustment to the expected price is regarded as a weighted average of past errors of prediction, and the weights decline backwards in time (op. cit., p. 59). No attempt is made, however, to relate this hypothesis to equilibrium in the model, and Brennan's remarks seem to indicate that he takes it for granted that equilibrium will always be achieved.[3]

How then is the problem of attainment of equilibrium to be treated?

Formally, a condition such as the following would suffice:

a $ED = 0$, where $ED =$ demand for storage less supply of storage

b $\dfrac{\partial ED}{\partial (P_{t+1} - P_t)} < 0$

There are various adjustment mechanisms which we may introduce to fulfil this condition. The first such mechanism is that, if the supply of storage were initially $0M$, we may assume that suppliers always expect the price change of the current period to continue, and adjust their quantities of storage accordingly. In this way, a cobweb would be set up, which would converge to equilibrium if the usual conditions were met (see R. G. D. Allen, *Mathematical Economics*, London, 1964, chapter 1).

Second, suppose expectations are formed according to an

adaptive expectations hypothesis,[4] where the revision of expectations for the next period is a proportion of the error in the expectation for the current period:

$$E(P_{t+1}) - E(P_t) = \beta\{P_t - E(P_t)\} \tag{4.6}$$

that is,

$$E(P_{t+1}) = (1 - \beta)E(P_t) + \beta P_t \tag{4.6a}$$
$$0 < \beta < 1$$

Equation (4.6a) can be shown, by successive substitution, to be equal to

$$E(P_{t+1}) = \beta P_t + \beta(1 - \beta)P_{t-1} +$$
$$\beta(1 - \beta)^2 P_{t-2} + \ldots \tag{4.7}$$

which can be written as

$$E(P_{t+1}) = \beta \sum_{i=0}^{\infty} (1 - \beta)^i P_{t-i} \tag{4.7a}$$

If expectations are revised in this way, then, given the supply and demand functions, equilibrium will eventually be reached, since the weights given to past prices decline geometrically as we go back in time.[5]

Brennan's revision of expectations model is a type of adaptive expectations hypothesis. He writes $P^*(t)_{t+1}^n$ for the series of $(n - t)$ expected spot prices (adjusted for transitory factors) formed in month t (op. cit., p. 59). This series contains all expected spot prices from period $t + 1$ to period n. Similarly $P^*(t - 1)_{t+1}^n$ represents a series of $(n - t)$ expected prices, relating to periods $t + 1$ to n, and formed in month $t - 1$.

The adjustment to expectations for transitory factors, made in period t, is expressed as a weighted average of past errors, with declining weights for past time periods:

$$P^*(t)_{t+1}^n - P^*(t - 1)_{t+1}^n = \alpha\{P_t - E(P_t)\} +$$
$$\alpha(1 - \alpha)\{P_{t-1} - E(P_{t-1})\} +$$
$$\alpha(1 - \alpha)^2\{P_{t-2} - E(P_{t-2})\} + \ldots \tag{4.8}$$

where $0 < \alpha < 1$.

Expectations revised in this way will tend to lead to the achievement of equilibrium in the way described above.

Third, suppose expectations are regressive with respect to the amount of the price change:[6]

$$E(P_{t+1}) - P_t = \alpha - \beta(P_t - P_{t-1}) \qquad (4.9)$$

If, for example, $\alpha = 0$ and $\beta = 1$, and if the amount of the current price rise is $0T$, then stockholders expect the price to fall in the next period by an amount $|0T|$. They will reduce the supply of storage, and the actual price rise will be larger than before. Clearly, however, whether equilibrium will be reached by this method depends on the values of α and β; for example, if $\alpha = 0R$ and $\beta < 1$ equilibrium will eventually be reached.

Thus, it is necessary to introduce an adjustment mechanism (of which three examples only are given here) for expectations and hence supply of storage, to deal with cases where the actual price change is not equal to the expected price change.

A further disadvantage of this model is that the achievement of equilibrium in any meaningful sense appears to require that individuals have identical mean expectations. (For a theory which attempts to take into account heterogeneous expectations, see chapter 7.)

The individual's supply of storage curve m_t is the locus of equilibria for the individual: that is, it gives values of S_t where $E(P_{t+1}) - P_t = m_t$ ($E(P_{t+1})$ is taken to be the individual's mean spot price expectation). As expectations change, the individual moves along his supply function.

If all individuals have the same mean expectation $0R$, then g_t gives the sum of individual quantities of storage $0L$, at that expected price. Equilibrium will be immediately achieved.

Suppose, however, that individuals have different expectations, that $0R$ is a weighted average of individuals' mean expectations, and that $0L$ is the quantity of storage forth-

E

coming. If the demand curve passes through ($0L$, $0R$), $0R$ would be called the equilibrium price change. Yet the model is not necessarily in equilibrium, because all firms whose mean expected price change is not $0R$, although maximizing expected net revenue, are not maximizing realized net revenue.

Firms whose expected price change is less than $0R$, we may suppose, will increase their supplies of storage (depending on the adjustment mechanism assumed); firms whose expected price change exceeds $0R$ will reduce their supplies of storage. There is no reason why the increases should counterbalance the decreases. Firms are likely to have different marginal net cost-of-storage functions, especially as this function contains two subjective variables, marginal risk premium and marginal convenience yield. Any consequent change in the market supply of storage means that this quantity is not in equilibrium.

Telser's model of futures prices

The second part of Telser's article contains a model which is concerned with the determination of the forward price. This is not an extension of the previous model to analyse the simultaneous determination of spot and futures prices, but is a separate model.

There are two main categories of operator in this model: 'hedgers' and 'speculators'. Hedgers may be either 'short' or 'long'. A short hedger is one who has bought stocks spot; his risk is that the spot price will fall. He can reduce[7] this risk by selling futures. A long hedger is one who has sold the finished product forward, and whose risk is that the spot price of raw materials will rise. He can reduce this risk by purchasing futures of the raw material.

Speculators in futures may also be either 'short' or 'long'. A long speculator expects the forward price to rise and buys futures. A short speculator expects the forward price to fall and so sells futures.

54

The model is first developed with speculators only.

p is the current futures price.
p'_i is the futures price expected by the ith speculator.
x_i represents the net purchases of futures by the ith speculator.

If $p > p'_i$, the ith speculator sells futures; if $p < p'_i$ he buys futures. Then excess demand by the ith speculator is a decreasing function of $(p - p_i)$

$$x_i = a_i(p - p'_i) \tag{4.9}$$

where $a_i < 0$ (ibid., p. 239).

For the futures price to be in equilibrium it is necessary that purchases of futures by speculators equal sales of futures by speculators, i.e. that $\Sigma x_i = 0$. In a two-period model the expected futures price is the same as the expected spot price. The equilibrium futures price is regarded as a weighted average of expected spot prices of all speculators. This is shown as follows (ibid., p. 240, n. 8).

The individual's excess demand function is

$$x_i = a_i(p - p'_i) \tag{4.10}$$

The equilibrium condition for p is that $\Sigma x_i = 0$; that is

$$\Sigma a_i(p - p_i) = 0$$

Therefore

$$p = \frac{\Sigma a_i p_i}{\Sigma a_i} \tag{4.11}$$

The market excess demand function is:

$$\Sigma x_i = \Sigma a_i(p - p'_i)$$

That is

$$p = \frac{\Sigma x_i}{\Sigma a_i} + \frac{\Sigma a_i p'_i}{\Sigma a_i} \tag{4.12}$$

This is a straight line by assumption (loc. cit.) with a negative gradient, $\frac{1}{\Sigma a_i}$. However, as the number of speculators tends to ∞, $\frac{1}{\Sigma a_i} \longrightarrow 0$; so that when the number of speculators is very large, the excess demand curve differs imperceptibly from the horizontal.

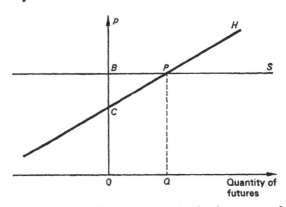

Figure 3 Price determination in the futures market
(from L. G. Telser, 1958)

Market excess demand is given by the curve S in Figure 3. The equilibrium futures price OB has the value $\frac{\Sigma a_i p_i'}{\Sigma a_i}$.

The position of the S curve would appear to depend on:

a The expectations of individuals
b The series $a_1, a_2, \ldots, a_i \ldots$ which reflects the strength of individuals' reactions to their expectations. This apparently depends on such things as the variance of the individual's expectations, his psychological reaction to risk and his capital. The nature of the functional relationship given by a_i, however, is not discussed by Telser, and is assumed linear

Telser points out that if all speculators have the same expectations, $p = p_i'$ for all i. Then $x_i = 0$ for all i, so that there would be no trading. Disagreement, he says, is essential to speculation (loc. cit.). This differs from the treatment in the previous models where identical expectations are assumed. The critical difference is that in this model there are speculators only, whereas in the previous models there were two categories of operator, stockholders and consumers.

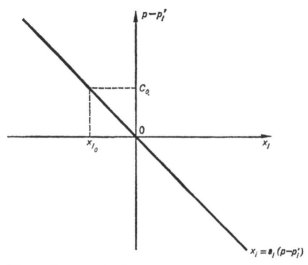

Figure 4   An individual speculator's market position

The horizontal axis in Figure 3 is labelled 'quantity of futures'. In fact it shows Σx_i: aggregate net purchases by speculators. The model does not give the total number of futures contracts exchanged on the market, but this is readily seen to be $\frac{1}{2}\Sigma|x_i|$.

Neither does the model give the equilibrium holding of futures contracts for the individual, although this is easily found. Suppose the ith speculator's expectations are such that $(p - p_i') = C_0$ (see Figure 4). He expects the futures price to fall and will sell a quantity of futures x_{i_0}.

Hedgers are then introduced to the model. Short hedgers

reduce the risk of a fall in the spot price by selling futures. From this, Telser argues that futures trading increases the quantity of stocks a firm is willing to hold for a given supply price of storage. (As we have seen, Telser defined the supply price of storage as $E(P) - P$, where P is the spot price. Op. cit., p. 236.) The long hedger reduces the risk of a rise in the spot price by buying futures. This is taken to mean that futures trading diminishes the quantity of stocks a firm will wish to hold at each supply price of storage.

The net effect on firms' total stockholding may go either way, and is called the 'excess supply of futures'. It is equal to the supply of futures by short hedgers less the demand for futures by long hedgers (ibid., pp. 240–1).

Given the spot price and expectations of hedgers, the excess supply of futures is an increasing function of the futures price. This is because, as the futures price rises, first, short hedging becomes more profitable, so that short hedgers will hold more stocks and sell more futures; and second, the cost of long hedging increases so that long hedgers buy less futures. This is shown as the function H in Figure 3. There will be some price $0C$ at which the supply by short hedgers equals the demand by long hedgers.

Telser's evidence (loc. cit., p. 240) indicates that hedgers are net short and speculators are net long, so that the inter-section of the S and H curves is to the right of the point $(0, 0)$. The excess supply of futures by hedgers ($0Q$) is equal to the excess demand for futures by speculators.

The equilibrium futures price is $0B$, as before. Thus hedgers do not influence the level of the futures price, which depends only on the expectations of speculators and the strength of their reactions to their expectations as given by the series $a_1, a_2, \ldots, a_i, \ldots$

The introduction of hedgers' expectations means that 'hedgers' are speculators of a type. For if short hedgers expect the spot price to rise they will not hedge; similarly long hedgers will not hedge if they expect the spot price to fall. Indeed, if short hedgers are predominantly bullish and long hedgers are predominantly bearish, there may be few hedgers operating as such. The H curve will shift to take into account the change in the net supply of futures by hedgers.

One of the ways in which hedgers may back their expectations is to under- or over-hedge.[8] To the extent that hedgers over-hedge (i.e. sell or buy more futures than they hold spot contracts) they may be counted as 'speculators' in Telser's sense. But to the extent that they under-hedge (i.e. sell or buy less futures than they hold spot contracts) a third category of operator, merchants or speculators in spot, is created. The introduction of this type of operator (or the amalgamation of this model with the storage model considered earlier in this chapter) therefore seems to be a necessary modification to this model.

Notes

1   Brennan follows Kaldor (*Essays*, pp. 21, 23, 26) regarding the shape of these functions and assumes $\sigma_t > 0$, $r'_t > 0$, $c'_t \geqslant 0$, and $\sigma''_t \geqslant 0$, $r''_t \geqslant 0$, $c''_t < 0$, whence $m'_t \gtrless 0$ and $m''_t > 0$. The marginal net cost of storage and its components are defined as functions of S_t, and the prime markings indicate partial derivatives with respect to S_t. The second-order condition for $E(NR)$ to be a maximum, that $m''_t > \partial E(MR)/\partial S_t$, will be satisfied under Brennan's assumptions.

2   Telser refers also to the persistence of firms in the industry (op. cit., pp. 237–8); however, it is possible for a firm to make a series of short-run losses, which is balanced by a series of short-run profits, and thus remain in the industry in the long run.

3   Ibid., pp. 56, 57. 'as production and planned inventories vary seasonally the demand curve will shift . . . we may reasonably assume that the supply curve of storage is relatively stable. If we allow demand to fluctuate over a stable supply function, a supply curve of storage can be generated empirically by measuring the relationship between $E(P_{t+1}) - P_t$ and S_t for $t = 1, 2, 3, \ldots, n$.'

4   See, for example, M. Nerlove, 'Adaptive Expectations and Cobweb Phenomena', *Quarterly Journal of Economics*, 1958, vol. 72, pp. 227–40, and A. Hirsch and M. C. Lovell, 'Structure of

Expectations', *Carnegie Institute of Technology Paper*, July 1967.

5 Alternatively one may say that the weights given to past errors of expectation decline geometrically backwards: for example, going back four periods,

$$E(P_{t+1}) = (1 - \beta)^4[E(P_{t-4}) - \beta\{E(P_{t-4}) - P_{t-4}\}]\beta(1 - \beta)^3 P_{t-3} \\ + \beta(1 - \beta)^2 P_{t-2} + \beta(1 - \beta)P_{t-1} + \beta P_t.$$

6 See, for example, A. Hirsch and M. C. Lovell, op. cit.

7 Telser, op. cit., p. 241. Although Telser speaks of 'avoiding' this risk (p. 240), it is clear that the later concept of hedging is used, for on p. 241 he states that hedgers substitute a basis risk for a price risk.

8 It would appear that hedgers may back their expectations by extending or curtailing the scope of their operations in spot and futures (either equally or unequally), by not hedging at all (with or without a change in spot transactions), or by simply under- or over-hedging.

5
Theories of individual equilibrium: Jerome L. Stein

In the first part of his article, 'Simultaneous Determination of Spot and Futures Prices' (*American Economic Review*, 1961, vol. 51, pp. 1012–25), Stein is concerned with explaining the allocation of an individual's stockholding between hedged and unhedged stocks. This is done by postulating that the individual has an indifference map between the variables expected return and risk, and, by deriving an opportunity locus, giving expected return as a function of risk in relation to hedged and unhedged stock. Individual equilibrium is then determined as a tangency solution.

He then develops a technique for the determination of spot and futures prices. This is done by deriving the conditions for equilibrium in the storage and futures markets, at first separately and then simultaneously.

The expected return per unit on unhedged stocks is written as

$$u = p^* - p - m \qquad (5.1)$$

where p^* is the individual's expected spot price (the mean of his subjective probability function of expected spot prices)
p is the current spot price
m is the marginal net carrying costs (assumed to be an increasing function of stocks held, ibid., p. 1013).

The expected return per unit on hedged stocks is

$$h = (p^* - p - m) - (q^* - q)$$
$$= u - (q^* - q) \tag{5.2}$$

where q^* is the individual's expected futures price
q is the current futures price.

The hedging procedure used is:

> At t_1 the stockholder buys stocks spot and hedges by selling futures contracts
> At t_2 he sells the stocks spot and closes his futures position by buying futures contracts equal to the number initially sold.

The expected gain on spot transactions is $p^* - p - m$; the expected loss on transactions in futures is $(q^* - q)$.

If at t_2 it costs more to buy back the futures contracts than is received from the spot sale (i.e. if the realized value of q^* exceeds the realized value of p^*), then the goods will be delivered under the futures contract. That is, although a loss is possible with hedged stocks, this loss is limited at $(q - p - m)$, which is the cost of delivering the goods (ibid., p. 1014).

As a measure of the risk involved Stein uses the variance of expected return, and assumes that the distributions of p^* and q^* are symmetrical. This makes the variance a more efficient measure of risk than if the distributions were skewed. This procedure follows J. Tobin, 'Liquidity Preference as Behaviour Toward Risk', *Review of Economic Studies*, 1957–8, vol. 25, p. 72.

For unhedged stocks the risk is $V(u) = V(p^*)$, and for hedged stocks it is $V(h) = V(p^*) + V(q^*) - 2 \operatorname{Cov}(p^* q^*)$.

The variance, however, I suggest, is only an indicator of the risk involved, and not a precise measure of this risk when prices change with expectations given. For example, let us compare two situations where the individual holds unhedged stocks. The subjective risk of loss is the probability that the spot price will fall, which will be different in the two situations if the spot price were different (given the individual's expectations). If the spot price were p_0, the risk would be $\int_{E_1}^{p_0} f(p^*)\, dp^*$, while if the spot price were $p_1(>p_0)$, the risk would be $\int_{E_1}^{p_1} f(p^*)\, dp^*$, (where $E_2 - E_1$ is the range of p^*, and $f(p^*)$ is the individual's distribution of expected spot prices). The risk, however, as indicated by $V(p^*)$ would appear to be constant. (On p. 1014 of his article Stein mentions, but dismisses, the 'probability of loss' as a measure of risk. The variance is, of course, an efficient measure of risk when the variance changes with mean expectation and prices given.)

The question is then: What proportion of the individual's stock is to be hedged?

In Figure 5, expected return is shown on the $0y$ axis, while risk and the proportion of stock unhedged are shown on $0x$.

There is first an opportunity locus HU which gives risk as a function of expected return for various percentages of unhedged stock. When all stock is hedged, the expected return is h, and the risk is $V(h)$. When all stock is unhedged the expected return is u and the risk is $V(u)$. As the percentage of stock unhedged varies from 0 to 100, the expected return varies from h to u. Unhedged stock is assumed to give a higher expected return and to involve a higher risk than hedged stock, so that HU has a positive slope (ibid., p. 1015). Moreover, the opportunity locus has a negative second derivative on the assumption that unhedged stock yields a greater expected return than hedged stock.[1]

Second, there is a set of indifference curves which are iso-expected utility curves. These curves have a positive gradient which implies that expected return yields an expected utility

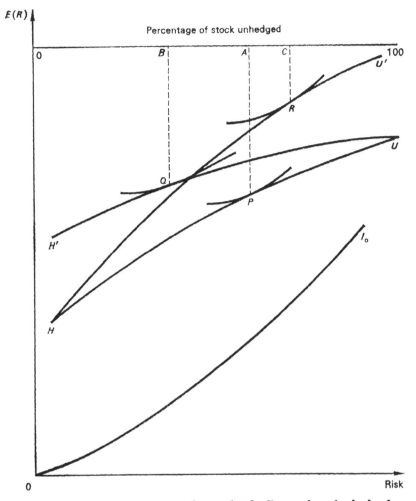

Figure 5   The proportion of an individual's stock to be hedged
(from J. L. Stein, 1961)

and risk an expected disutility. Stein says nothing about the individual's attitude to risk: whether he is risk-loving in the sense that risk yields an expected utility.

It would appear, however, that the assumption that risk yields an expected disutility is essential to Stein's argument

64

as stated. For he says that if HU had a negative gradient (that is, if hedged stock gave a higher expected return than unhedged stock) no unhedged stocks would be carried (op. cit., p. 1015): the highest indifference curve would be attained at the $0y$ axis. If the indifference curves had a negative slope, however, equilibrium would be possible in the $x0y$ plane and some percentage of unhedged stocks would be carried.[2]

The indifference curves are convex down on the assumption that the marginal utility of income is falling. This also implies that the marginal disutility of risk is not falling faster than the marginal utility of income, otherwise the indifference curves would be convex up.

Equilibrium for the individual is given by tangency of HU to the indifference curve at P, and $0A$ is the proportion of stock unhedged.[3]

Stein then considers the effect of an increase in the futures price *ceteris paribus*. This raises the expected return on hedged stock, but leaves the expected return on unhedged stock unchanged. The opportunity locus pivots on U to become $H'U$, and the new equilibrium is at Q.

The movement to the new equilibrium is said to be the result of, first, the substitution effect: the proportion of unhedged stock tends to decline because the increase in the futures price makes hedging more attractive (ibid., p. 1016). Second, there is the income effect. Stein explains that the higher expected utility made possible by the increase in q 'may affect the individual's aversion to risk' (loc. cit.); he becomes willing to take more risk at a given expected return as expected utility increases. Hence the income effect tends to increase the proportion of unhedged stock. The substitution effect dominates so that the proportion of unhedged stock falls.

This result is true for the quadratic utility function assumed by Stein (following Tobin, op. cit., p. 79), but need not necessarily follow. The income effect is a movement to another indifference curve, brought about by a change which alters h and u equally—for example, a change in the spot price or in the marginal net carrying cost. In the general case this effect may operate in favour of hedged stock or unhedged stock (if risk were an 'inferior discommodity'), or may leave the proportion of unhedged stock unchanged. Thus generally, where the proportion of unhedged stock decreases, it is not possible to say prima facie whether the income effect is reinforcing the substitution effect, or is operating in the opposite direction, but is outweighed by the substitution effect.

Stein's statement that the higher expected utility 'may affect the individual's aversion to risk' means here that the indifference curves become flatter as E rises at any given R, and is based on the utility function he assumes. (No change in the indifference map is implied.)

Consider next the effect of an equal increase in p^* and q^*. This leaves h unaltered, but u increases; HU pivots upward on H to become HU'. The new equilibrium is at R. In this case the income and substitution effects operate in the same direction; the rise in p^* will make unhedged stock more attractive (substitution effect) and the increase in expected utility will mean that the individual becomes willing to take more risk at any given expected return (income effect).

The other question, which is logically prior to that of what proportion to hedge, is whether to sell the stock spot (or forward) or supply storage.

Stein's argument is that the individual should supply storage if the expected utility from stockholding exceeds the utility from a spot sale (op. cit., p. 1016).[4] He takes the indifference curve I_0, passing through $(0, 0)$, the valuation of which is the utility from a spot sale. This is compared with the maximum expected utility from stockholding as given at the point of equilibrium P. If P is on a higher indifference curve than I_0 then the stock is carried over; if not, it is sold spot.

It should be pointed out that storage yields an expected utility, while a spot sale yields a realized utility. Although the two are not the same thing, apparently the individual is assumed to translate one into the other in order to compare the valuation of I_0 with that of the curve on which P lies.

Stein's market theory

Although this chapter is concerned with a theory of individual equilibrium, it seems appropriate to include a note on Stein's market theory, which is related to his theory of the individual.

In this theory two markets are distinguished, the storage market and that for futures. The link between these markets is the supply of hedged storage, which equals the supply of futures contracts, the latter being taken up by long speculators in the futures market.

The link between this theory and the theory of the individual, discussed above, is the total supply of storage, which is defined as the demand for stocks by the owners of stocks, and is a direct function of the individual's maximum expected utility as given by the indifference map equilibrium.

The supply of storage comprises the supply of unhedged storage and of hedged storage, and is written

$$S_D = U(p^* - p - m) + H(p^* - q^* + b - m) \qquad (5.3)$$

where $b = q - p$, and $U', H' > 0$ (Stein, op. cit., p. 1017). (The transition from the individual's supply to the market supply of storage is not discussed, but one may regard the market supply as the sum of individual supplies, on the assumption that there are no economies or diseconomies of storage.)

This function is quite orthodox in that, first, the demand for unhedged stocks is an inverse function of the spot price,

67

and second, the supply of hedged storage is a direct function of contango, given expectations and the marginal net carrying cost.

p^* and q^* refer to the 'average expectations appropriately weighted', of all individuals (ibid., pp. 1017–18). No explicit assumption is made about the homogeneity or otherwise of expectations, but unless expectations are identical, p^* and q^* are not the same as the individual's mean expected prices referred to above.

The quantity of stocks held by the individual is an increasing function of the individual's maximum expected utility, but this quantity is not determined by the theory. Therefore, although the proportion of stock to be hedged by each individual is known, the quantity of futures contracts supplied by him is not known.

Although the theory of the individual is initially developed for a short hedger (such a short hedger is, of course, a hedger-speculator in terms of the definitions of chapter 2, and corresponds to the 'mixed trader' category of Peston and Yamey), it is subsequently generalized to cover the case of long hedging. The position of the long hedger is said to be the negative of that of the short hedger. This is meant presumably in the sense, first that the long hedger is short of the commodity, and second, that his risk is that the spot price of the commodity will rise. The generalization is completed by regarding the quantity of the finished commodity to be sold forward by the long hedger as a function of his maximum expected utility.

The demand for storage is defined to be the quantity of stocks in existence, and equals the opening stocks of the period S_{-1}, plus the excess of current production over current consumption $X = X(p, a)$ where a is a parameter such that $\partial X / \partial a > 0$.

Hence the demand for storage function is:

$$S_S = S_{-1} + X(p, a) \tag{5.4}$$

All stocks in existence must be held by someone, so it would appear that stockholders provide both the supply of and demand for storage. The spot price, however, is still a competitively determined market price, because of the influence of consumption demand. (In this context, the Peston and Yamey method seems preferable, since it avoids this apparent difficulty. They distinguish the market for present consumption from the other two, and introduce a separate function 'demand for hedged storage' by long speculators.)

Equilibrium in the storage market requires

$$U(p^* - p - m) + H(p^* - q^* + b - m) =$$
$$S_{-1} + X(p, a) \qquad (5.5)$$

A large range of values of p and b will permit this equilibrium, and to obtain the locus of (b, p) values required, Stein differentiates (5.5) with respect to p and solves for $\partial b / \partial p$. Thus (Stein, op. cit., p. 1019)

$$\frac{\partial U}{\partial p} + \frac{\partial H}{\partial b} \cdot \frac{\partial b}{\partial p} = \frac{\partial X}{\partial p}$$

so that

$$\frac{\partial b}{\partial p} = \frac{X'_p - U'_p}{H'_b}$$

which is positive, since $X'_p > 0$, $U'_p < 0$ and $H'_b > 0$.

So S, the locus of (b, p) values representing equilibrium in the storage market, has a positive gradient.

The supply of futures is equal to the supply of hedged storage, and is therefore represented by the function

$$S_F = H(p^* - q^* + b - m) \qquad (5.6)$$

Hedgers are assumed to be net short in futures, and the demand is provided by long speculators whose expected futures price is q'. The demand function for futures is

$$D_F = G(q' - q)$$
$$= G(q' - b - p) \qquad (5.7)$$

where $G' > 0$.

F

Equilibrium in this market requires

$$H(p^* - q^* + b - m) = G(q' - b - p) \qquad (5.8)$$

The locus F of (b, p) values giving equilibrium in the futures market is obtained as before.

$$\frac{\partial H}{\partial b} \cdot \frac{\partial b}{\partial p} = \frac{-\partial G}{\partial b} \cdot \frac{\partial b}{\partial p} - \frac{\partial G}{\partial p}$$

Therefore

$$\frac{\partial b}{\partial p} = \frac{-G'_p}{H'_b + G'_b}$$

which is positive, since $G'_p < 0$, $H'_b > 0$ and $G'_b < 0$.

This locus, therefore, has a negative gradient.

Simultaneous equilibrium in the storage and futures markets is represented by the intersection of the two loci, S and F. Full equilibrium of the spread and spot price is given by the coordinates of that intersection, (b_0, p_0): the equilibrium futures price is, of course, $b_0 + p_0$.

To be meaningful, this equilibrium price spread must conform to the arbitrage constraint $q \leqslant p + m$. It would seem that this condition will be fulfilled although it is not explicitly introduced by Stein. Stein points out that the limit to the loss on hedged stocks is $q - p - m$, but this limit is operative only when it is more profitable to deliver the commodity, rather than close the futures position by reversal (see chapter 5, above). The inequality $q \leqslant p + m$, however, must hold for the market at all times (assuming that m represents all the marginal costs of arbitrage). We can assume that the arbitrage function is performed by 'hedgers', so that the supply of 'hedged storage' will expand accordingly whenever a riskless profit can be earned.

Notes

1 Stein, 'The Opportunity Locus in a Hedging Decision: A Correction', *American Economic Review*, 1964, vol. 54, pp. 762–3.

In this note, Stein explains that the total risk of any market position is

$$R = V[xu + (1 - x)h]$$
$$= V[p^* - (1 - x)q^*]$$
$$= \sigma_p^2 + (1 - x)^2\sigma_q^2 - 2(1 - x)r\sigma_p\sigma_q$$

where x is the proportion of stock unhedged, $\sigma_p^2 = V(p^*)$ and $\sigma_q^2 = V(q^*)$.

The expected return from any market position is $E = xu + (1 - x)h$.

The slope of the opportunity locus is

$$\frac{dE}{dR} = \frac{dE}{dx}\bigg/\frac{dR}{dx}$$

$$= \frac{u - h}{2(-\sigma_q^2 + x\sigma_q^2 + r\sigma_p\sigma_q)}$$

Then

$$\frac{d^2E}{dR^2} = \frac{E_x''R' - R_x''E_x}{(R_x')^2}$$

$$= \frac{-\sigma_q^2(u - h)}{2\{(1 - x)\sigma_q^2 - r\sigma_p\sigma_q\}^2}$$

which is <0 when $u > h$.

2   Thus the model can easily be modified to handle the case of a risk-lover. The indifference curves for such an individual would have a negative slope: if HU had a negative slope an equilibrium may occur in the $x0y$ plane, but if HU had a positive slope no *hedged* stocks would be carried.

3   In the original paper, the opportunity locus was presented as linear, so that convexity of the indifference curves was a necessary condition of equilibrium. Once downward concavity of the opportunity locus is established, however, the condition is that prior to the point of tangency the indifference curve has a smaller, and afterwards a greater gradient than HU.

4   Certainty may be obtained by selling the stock spot or forward. If $p \neq q - m$, then sale at one price yields a higher utility than sale at the other. It would appear that it is the method of sale giving rise to the higher utility, which is relevant to the valuation of the curve I_0.

6
Theories of individual equilibrium: Leland L. Johnson

Johnson's aim is to develop a theory to explain the individual's market position in spot and futures contracts, incorporating both hedging and speculative elements ('The Theory of Hedging and Speculation in Commodity Futures', *Review of Economic Studies*, June 1960, pp. 139–51).

None of the other major theories considered here treats this problem in the same way as Johnson. Of the theories published prior to Johnson's, Keynes treats the hedger as a pure hedger who always takes a full hedge, without reference to his price expectations. In Working, while the hedging and speculative elements are incorporated, the position is said to be taken according to the expectation of a change in the *basis*. There is no explanation of positions which may be taken according to expectations of changes in the absolute level of spot and futures prices. Brennan and Telser make the individual's stockholding a function of the expected change in the spot price, and Telser then treats hedgers and speculators in the futures market as separate groups.

Of the theories published simultaneously with or after Johnson, that of Peston and Yamey is essentially a market analysis, while Stein's determines explicitly the proportion of the individual's stockholding to be hedged, taking speculative and hedging elements into account, but does not determine the actual holding of spot and futures contracts.

73

Assume that the individual's expectation of a price change in the ith market is represented by a subjective probability density function with mean u_i and variance σ_i^2. Using the variance as a measure of risk, the price risk of holding x units in the ith market is $x_i^2 \sigma_i^2$.

Similarly, his expected price change in the jth market is represented by a subjective probability density function with mean u_j and variance σ_j^2. The risk associated with a holding of x units in the jth market is $x_j^2 \sigma_j^2$.

Hence the total risk for an individual with positions in both markets is:

$$V(R) = x_i^2 \sigma_i^2 + x_j^2 \sigma_j^2 + 2x_i\, x_j \operatorname{Cov}_{ij} \qquad (6.1)$$

Use of the variance as a measure of risk is here subject to the same criticisms as were made in chapter 5.

The expected return for an individual with positions in both markets is:

$$E(R) = x_i u_i + x_j u_j \qquad (6.2)$$

The ith market is regarded as the primary market. A hedge is defined as a position (x_j^*) in the jth market which minimizes the price risk, given the position in the ith market.

To find x_j^*, differentiate (6.1) with respect to x_j:

$$\frac{\partial V(R)}{\partial x_j} = 2x_j\, \sigma_j^2 + 2x_i \operatorname{Cov}_{ij}$$

$$= 0 \quad \text{for } V(R) \quad \text{a minimum (first-order condition).}[1]$$

Therefore

$$x_j^* = \frac{-x_i \operatorname{Cov}_{ij}}{\sigma_j^2} \qquad (6.3)$$

Hence the minimum risk $V(R)^*$ is found by substituting in (6.1) for x_j:

$$V(R)^* = x_i^2 \sigma_i^2 - \frac{x_i^2 \operatorname{Cov}_{ij}^2}{\sigma_j^2}$$

$$= x_i^2 \sigma_i^2 (1 - \rho^2) \qquad (6.4)$$

where $\rho = \text{Cov}_{ij}/\sigma_i\sigma_j$ is the coefficient of correlation between the expected price changes (Johnson, op. cit., p. 143).

Johnson says that if the expected price changes are perfectly correlated $\rho^2 = 1$ and the overall risk is zero. (The risk is zero, of course, only if the correlation is positive.) If the individual believes there is no correlation between the expected price changes $\rho^2 = 0$, and $V(R) = x_i^2 \sigma_i^2$ which is the price risk in the ith market.

The effectiveness e of the hedge is measured by the ratio of $V(R)^*$, the minimum total price risk, to the price risk in the ith market:

$$e = 1 - \frac{V(R)^*}{x_i^2 \sigma_i^2}$$

Therefore

$$e = \rho^2 \tag{6.5}$$

The higher the value of e, the more effective the hedge ($0 \leqslant e \leqslant 1$). Hence the effectiveness of hedging is measured in subjective terms.

As Johnson states, however, this is a measure only of the extent to which the hedge is expected to be effective. I suggest that nothing is gained by this measure. Johnson certainly does not claim any advantages for this subjective version. The effectiveness of hedging would appear to be better measured in *ex post* terms, because whether a hedge is effective can only be decided when the outcome is known.

On the other hand it would appear preferable to specify price risk in subjective terms, because it is the trader's evaluation of this risk which is relevant to his decision-making.

Johnson assumes that the aim of the individual is to find the optimum combination of risk and expected return, subject to the constraint of risk minimization in the primary market, as developed above.

75

The positions open to the individual are assumed to be:

a   Long in spot, the ith market. At this stage of the analysis Johnson assumes that a merchandising profit of m per unit is also earned in this market

b   Short in futures, the jth market

c   Long in futures.

Futures positions are assumed to be closed out by reversing the transaction at the relevant later date. No short positions in spot are postulated.

The expected return for such an individual is

$$E(R) = x_i(u_i + m) + x_j u_j \qquad (6.6)$$

Johnson assumes that the individual's preferences are represented by an indifference map between the variables expected return $E(R)$ and risk $\sqrt{V(R)}$. The marginal rate of substitution of expected return for risk is assumed to fall.

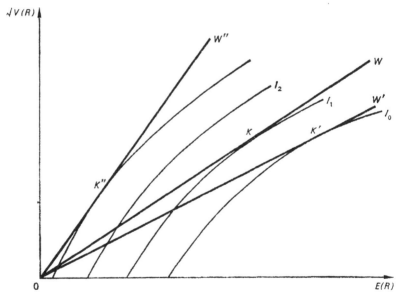

Figure 6(a)   Determination of an individual's spot and futures market positions (from L. L. Johnson, 1959–60)

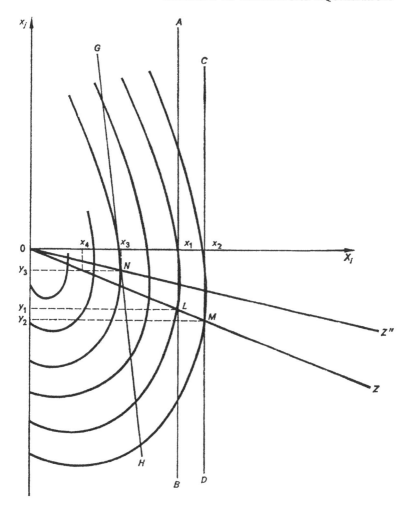

Figure 6(b)   Determination of an individual's spot and futures market positions (from L. L. Johnson, 1959–60)

The positive gradient of the indifference curves implies that risk yields an expected disutility and expected return an expected utility: the individual is a risk-averter in this sense. In Figure 6(a) the curve I_0 is preferred to I_1 and higher curves.

77

Within the context of the problem, equation (6.1)

$$V(R) = x_i^2 \, \sigma_i^2 + x_j^2 \, \sigma_j^2 + 2x_i \, x_j \, \mathrm{Cov}_{ij}$$

is an ellipse with centre (0, 0) and major axis rotated through an angle

$$\tfrac{1}{2} \operatorname{arcot} \left(\frac{\sigma_i^2 - \sigma_j^2}{2 \, \mathrm{Cov}_{ij}} \right)$$

given $V(R)$ and the individual's expectations.[2] For different values of $V(R)$ there is a series of concentric ellipses, with centre (0, 0), axes x_i, x_j, and located in the first and fourth quadrants.

Equation (6.6) is represented by a series of iso-expected return lines with gradient

$$\frac{\partial x_j}{\partial x_i} = -\frac{(u_i + m)}{u_j}$$

If $u_i = u_j = 0$ there is a series of vertical iso-$E(R)$ lines AB, CD and so on (see Figure 6(b)). In this case $E(R)$ depends on m, and therefore depends on the x_i position only. CD indicates a higher expected return than AB, given m.

In Figure 6(b), $0Z$ is the locus of tangencies of iso-$E(R)$ lines with ellipses of constant risk, and must be linear (Johnson, op. cit., p. 147). Tangency represents the market position of minimum risk at a given $E(R)$. In this way the minimum risk condition developed above is used.

The valuation of the iso-risk and iso-expected return lines is cardinal, and refers to known quantities. The valuation of the indifference curves in Figure 6(a) is, of course, ordinal only.

If the combinations of expected return and risk given by $0Z$ (Figure 6(b)) are plotted in Figure 6(a) the opportunity locus $0W$ results, which must also be linear (ibid.). The optimum combination of risk and expected return is given at K, the point of tangency between $0W$ and I_1.

The individual's market position is found by transferring the coordinates of K to Figure 6(b); this is at L, (x_1, y_1).

78

At L, (x_1, y_1) in Figure 6(b), y_1 corresponds to x_j^* in equation (6.3). Therefore

$$y_1 = \frac{-x_1 \, \text{Cov}_{ij}}{\sigma_j^2}$$

The gradient of $0Z = \dfrac{y_1}{x_1} = \dfrac{-\text{Cov}_{ij}}{\sigma_j^2}$

$$= -\rho \frac{\sigma_i}{\sigma_j}$$

Hence, $0Z$ gives the ordinate which constitutes a hedge for any given position in the spot market.

Suppose $u_i > 0$, $u_j = 0$. The iso-expected return lines remain vertical, but any given line represents a higher expected return than before. Although the locus of tangencies remains as $0Z$, when the risk-expected return combinations are transferred to Figure 6(a), the expected return at any given risk is higher than before. The opportunity locus becomes $0W'$, with equilibrium at K'. Both risk and expected return are higher than before. Transferring these values (at K') to Figure 6(b) results in the market position M, (x_2, y_2).

The individual's holding of spot is said to increase because a rise in the spot price is expected. Sales of futures increase as a hedge against the increase in spot (ibid., p. 148).

Johnson analyses the change in market position as follows. Suppose a_0 is a position in either market when $u_i = u_j = 0$, and a_1 is a position in the same market when either u_i or u_j is non-zero. Then $a_1 - a_0$ is defined as a *direct* speculative element if it refers to the market in which the price change is expected, and as an *indirect* speculative element if it refers to the market in which no price change is expected.

Thus $x_2 - x_1$ is a direct speculative element; $y_2 - y_1$ is an indirect speculative element (ibid.).

I suggest that it is possible to distinguish effects similar to

79

the income and substitution effects of consumer theory. In the movement from K to K', expected return must increase, and risk may rise or fall. The 'substitution' effect may be described as follows: the expectation of a rise in the spot price makes the holding of spot more attractive than a position in futures. This tends to encourage substitution in favour of spot and against futures.

The 'income' effect: at any given market position on $0Z$ there is an increase in expected return (this is true for all market positions which include spot holdings). In terms of the previous level of expectations, this is equivalent to a movement along $0Z$. This tends to encourage an increase in both spot and futures positions.

For spot the 'income' and 'substitution' effects work in the same direction, and for futures they work in opposite directions. In this case the 'income' effect dominates since both spot and futures positions increase, and the individual is on a higher risk ellipse.

Suppose, however, that a rise in the futures price only is expected:

$$u_i = 0, \qquad u_j > 0$$

The iso-expected return lines have a negative gradient, like GH in Figure 6(b) (ibid.). The locus of tangencies becomes $0Z''$. At any given market position (x_i, x_j), and thus at any given risk, expected return is now less than before, because a loss is expected on futures contracts. Therefore in Figure 6(a) the opportunity locus becomes $0W''$, with equilibrium at K''. Both risk and expected return are less than at K, and the market position is N, (x_3, y_3).

Diagrammatically, both spot and futures positions must decline because the individual is on an ellipse of lower risk, and the gradient of the ellipse at the point of intersection with $0Z''$ is negative.

In terms of the 'substitution' effect, the expected rise in the futures price makes short positions in futures relatively less attractive than spot holdings. This tends to increase spot holdings and reduce short futures positions. In terms of the 'income' effect, the reduction in expected return at any given market position tends to reduce both spot and futures positions (it is equivalent to a movement back along $0Z$ in terms of the old expectations). For futures the 'income' and 'substitution' effects work in the same direction. For spot they operate in opposite directions and the income effect dominates.

In the new market position N (x_3, y_3) a full hedge is not carried. A partial hedge is carried to reduce the price risk in spot, even though a loss is expected on the short position in futures (ibid.). In Figure 6(b), if the spot holding x_3 were carried unhedged the individual would be on an ellipse of higher risk. The hedge y_3 is sufficient to cover a long spot position x_4; $x_3 - x_4$ is unhedged.

It is clear from Figure 6(b) that if a large rise in the futures price were expected, so that the gradient of GH was a small negative quantity, the locus of tangencies would be in the first quadrant. The individual would then go long in futures.

In Johnson's terminology, the reduction in spot from x_1 to x_3 is an indirect speculative element; the reduction in futures from y_1 to y_3 is a direct speculative element (ibid.).

A change in the mean, variance or covariance of expectations, or in the merchandising profit m, will change the position of the opportunity locus in Figure 6(a).

The question is whether this will also cause a change in the value of expected utility represented by an indifference curve? If so, then it may not be possible to compare two equilibria in Figure 6(a); that is, one may not be able to say that the individual is better off simply because he is on a lower indifference curve.

I believe that the answer to this question is in the negative, and that the indifference curve technique is a legitimate tool for this situation.

I suggest that the shape and valuation of the indifference map depend on the individual's psychology alone. It tells one that with this much expected return and this much risk he would value the situation as worth a particular ordinal level of expected utility. If expected return were to increase by so much and risk were to increase by so much, he would be no better off and no worse off: the level of expected utility in the new situation would be the same as that in the previous situation, and he would be on the same indifference curve as before.

The indifference map represents a set of *hypothetical situations*; *if* expected return were so much, and *if* risk were so much, then expected utility *would* take some indicated ordinal level. Which of these situations is relevant at any particular time depends on the position of the opportunity locus.

The expected return on $0x$ obviously depends on the expected price changes and the market position, given the merchandising profit m. Any particular level of expected return, however, can be calculated by an infinite number of combinations of mean expectations and market positions. Similarly a given risk level can be calculated by an infinite number of combinations of market positions and variance and covariance of expectations.

So it is a change in the individual's psychology alone which can cause a change in the valuation of an indifference curve.

Of course, a change in the other parameters (u_i, u_j, σ_i^2, σ_j^2, Cov_{ij}) may react on the individual's psychology, and thereby cause a change in expected utility. The point is, however, that this is not a necessary consequence of such a change, and it is legitimate to assume that the indifference map is independent of the factors which affect the opportunity locus.

For this argument to hold it is important that the indifference map be drawn for the variables risk and expected return. If, on one of the axes spot or futures contracts were shown, then the expected utility from holding a particular number of contracts *would* depend on the expected price of that contract.

Johnson's paper deals with the determination of the individual's market position only, given the current spot and futures prices. He does not develop demand and supply functions for the individual for spot and futures contracts, nor does he deal with price determination in either market as a whole.

I suggest, however, that this can readily be done on the basis of his model for the individual. For example, an increase in the expected change in the spot price due to a change in expectations is equivalent to a fall in the current spot price given expectations of the level of that price. If spot purchases increase with an increase in the expected price change in spot (ibid., p. 148) *ceteris paribus*, this indicates that the individual's demand for spot contracts is a decreasing function of the spot price *ceteris paribus*.

Similarly, a rise in the expected change in the futures price due to an upward revision of expectations, with the current futures price given, is equivalent to a fall in the current futures price given expectations of the level of that price. Hence, if futures sales decline when there is a rise in the expected change in the futures price (ibid.) *ceteris paribus*, this indicates that the individual's supply of futures contracts varies directly with the futures price *ceteris paribus*.

Before it would be possible to proceed to price determination for the market as a whole, however, it would be necessary to introduce a group of traders who demand futures contracts, in the same price range that individuals represented by the model wish to sell. Similar assumptions would need to be made about the supply of the spot commodity.

No account is taken of an individual who is risk-loving in

the sense that risk yields a utility, although the indifference map (in Figure 6(*a*)) could be modified to do so as in Stein's model (see chapter 5 above). But the model could not deal satisfactorily with a risk-loving individual, with the present opportunity locus. Indifference curves with a negative gradient would not yield an equilibrium in the $x0y$ plane, nor on either axis.

Moreover, it would not be consistent to admit a risk-loving individual to this model, for one of the axioms in constructing the locus of tangencies in Figure 6(*b*) is that it represents positions of *minimum* risk at each expected return.

Notes

1   The second-order condition for $V(R)$ to be a minimum will be met so long as there is any price risk; that is

$$\frac{\partial^2 V(R)}{\partial x_j^2} = 4\sigma_j^2$$

which is >0 if $\sigma_j^2 > 0$.

2   A necessary condition for equation (6.1) to be represented by an ellipse is that

$$\text{Cov}_{ij}^2 - \sigma_i^2 \sigma_j^2 < 0$$

that is $\rho^2 - 1 < 0$.

Now $\rho^2 - 1$ must be $\leqslant 0$, since ρ^2 cannot be >1. If $\text{Cov}_{ij}^2 - \sigma_i^2 \sigma_j^2 = 0$, then equation (6.1) is a parabola, but in this case there is no optimization problem because $\rho^2 = 1$, and $V(R) = 0$.

7
Speculation in commodity futures: a method of analysis

Models of futures trading developed in recent years contain various unsatisfactory aspects: for example, Stein's model does not determine the quantity of stocks held by the individual; the models of Brennan and Telser assume identical expectations; that of Peston and Yamey does not deal with the determination of individual equilibrium, while that of Leland Johnson does not contain an analysis of market equilibrium.[1] The model developed here attempts to take account of these difficulties. The aim of this chapter is to develop a technique of analysis for speculation in commodity futures. The technique can also be used to analyse speculation in spot contracts, and hence to deal with the speculative element in positions of under- or over-hedging.[2]

The chapter starts with the determination of individual equilibrium, and then deals with the derivation of the individual speculator's demand and supply functions for futures contracts. The next two sections deal with the determination of equilibrium in the futures market assuming homogeneous and heterogeneous expectations respectively, while the following section is concerned with the application of the analysis to speculators forming expectations in terms of the price spread only. The final section deals with the simultaneous determination of spot and futures prices, where the market supply and demand functions are

G   85 derived according to the method discussed in the earlier sections.

Determination of individual equilibrium

Since the purpose of this chapter is to analyse speculation in commodity futures, the model developed here is restricted initially to a futures market with speculators only. The analysis is extended in the final section by introducing hedgers who are net short and speculation in spot.

The main assumptions of the model are as follows:

1 The individual's price expectations take the form of a subjective probability distribution $f(E)$, which is given.
2 The risk that the individual is willing to take that he is wrong in his market action $R(x)$, is some function of the size of his commitments x. (Extent of commitments is measured by the number of contracts bought or sold.) It is assumed that $R(x)$ can be specified in the range $0 \leqslant R(x) \leqslant 1$.
3 That there is some level of probability that his action is wrong (i.e. some level of futures price), at which he changes from buying to selling (or from selling to buying) futures.
4 That the individual determines his market position by equating: the probability that the price change will be against him, and the risk that he is willing to take that the price change will be against him.

In addition, some simplifying assumptions will be made:

a The function $f(E)$ is symmetrical with mean μ, and lies in the range E_1E_2.
b That the individual will not take a market position for which the subjective probability of an adverse price change is greater than 0·5: that is, $R(x)$ exists only in the range $0 \leqslant R(x) \leqslant 0·5$. If the current futures price $F < \mu$ he will buy futures; if $F > \mu$ he will sell futures.

(Generally the expected price at which the individual changes from buying to selling futures, or vice versa, will be denoted by E_m. In this case $E_m = \mu$.)

c That the function $R(x)$ is linear, and the individual has the same $R(x)$ function whether he is buying or selling futures.

d That we are concerned with two points of time only, t_0 and t_1. The expected price, E, means the expected spot price, and is the same as the expected price of a futures contract maturing at t_1. The price of such a future at t_1 will be the spot price at t_1 (ignoring costs of dealing). The individual is assumed to close out a futures contract by reversal of the transaction at maturity.

e The individual's capital is limited so that he can neither buy nor sell more than $0x_h$ futures contracts. When buying futures, it is assumed that the individual must pay a deposit at the time of purchase, and when selling that he must deposit a stake with the market authority at the time of sale, as a sign of good faith. Assumptions a, b, c and e will subsequently be relaxed.

The question is then: first, what quantity of futures contracts will the individual buy or sell for a given futures price, and second, what is the nature of the individual's demand and supply functions for futures?

If the current futures price were F_1, which is greater than μ (Figure 7(a)), the individual would sell futures. With a futures price F_1 the subjective probability that the price will rise is p_1, i.e. the risk of being wrong is p_1; (the risk of being wrong for a seller is given by the descending cumulative probability function $F(E)$). For a risk p_1, with downward sloping $R(x)$ curve, the individual will sell $0x_1$ futures contracts (Figure 7(b)). The point with coordinates (F_1, x_1) is therefore a point on the individual's supply curve.

If the individual had sold $0x_2$ futures contracts, he would

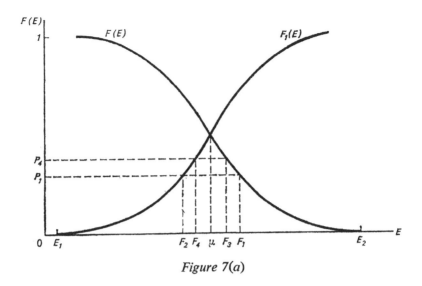

Figure 7(a)

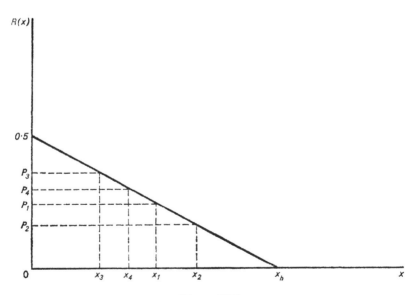

Figure 7(b)
Equilibrium for the individual speculator

not be in equilibrium. With commitments of $0x_2$, he is willing to take a risk of p_2. With a futures price F_1, however, he estimates the risk of loss as p_1, which exceeds the risk he is willing to take with commitments of that size. He is therefore induced to reduce his market commitments to $0x_1$, where the risk he is willing to take coincides with the risk which he estimates is involved in the current price situation. Similarly, the individual would not be in equilibrium if he had sold only $0x_3$ futures contracts. With commitments of $0x_3$ he is willing to take a risk of p_3, which is greater than that involved in the current price situation. He is therefore induced to expand his commitments to $0x_1$, where the risk he is willing to take is equal to p_1.

Similarly, if the futures price were F_4, which is less than μ, the individual would buy futures. For a futures price F_4 the subjective probability that the price will fall is p_4; i.e. the risk of being wrong is p_4 (the risk of being wrong for a buyer is given by the ascending cumulative probability function $F_1(E)$). For such a risk the individual is willing to buy $0x_4$ futures contracts. The point with coordinates (F_4, x_4) is therefore a point on the individual's demand curve.

Individual demand and supply functions

The question is then: what is the nature of the individual's supply and demand functions for futures contracts? In Figure 8 the vertical axis shows the current futures price minus the price at which the individual changes from buying to selling futures, i.e. $F - \mu$. On the horizontal axis, sales of futures contracts are shown; purchases are shown as negative sales. If $F > \mu$, the individual sells futures; therefore the supply curve lies in the first quadrant only. If $F < \mu$, the individual buys futures; therefore the demand curve lies in the third quadrant only.

In Figure 7(a), as the current futures price rises from μ to E_2, the probability of being wrong falls at a diminishing rate with respect to price. With a linear $R(x)$ function sales rise at a constant rate with respect to reductions in risk. Therefore sales rise at a diminishing rate with respect to increases in price. The supply curve slopes upward to the right and is concave up.

Similarly, as the current futures price falls from μ to E_1, the probability of being wrong falls at a diminishing rate

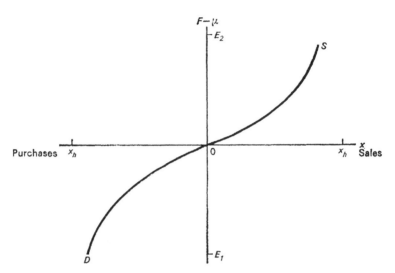

Figure 8   Demand for and supply of futures: risk-averting speculator

with respect to decreases in price. With linear $R(x)$, purchases rise at a constant rate with respect to falls in risk. Therefore purchases rise at a diminishing rate with respect to falls in price. The demand curve slopes downward to the left and is concave down. Both demand and supply curves exist only up to the ordinate at $0x_h$, the limit set by the capital constraint.

On the assumptions, the supply curve is a mirror image of the $F(E)$ curve below the value $F(E) = 0.5$, with axes rotated through π radians and contracts instead of probability on the horizontal axis. Similarly, the demand curve is a mirror

90

image of the $F_1(E)$ curve below $F_1(E) = 0.5$, with axes inverted and contracts purchased replacing probability.

This method may be used to derive demand and supply functions for an individual:

a Whose $R(x)$ function is constant
b Who is risk-loving in the sense that his $R(x)$ function slopes upward
c Who is inoperative for a particular price range because he requires the difference between the current futures price and μ to cover a risk premium
d Who changes from buying to selling futures at a price other than μ
e Who is risk-loving in the sense that he buys futures when $F > \mu$ and sells futures when $F < \mu$.

The first three of these cases will be discussed here, and the fourth is dealt with on pp. 96-7.

R(x) *function constant*[3]
Suppose that the individual's $R(x)$ function is constant at $R(x) = p_1$ (Figure 7(b)), and that he has the same $R(x)$ function whether he is buying or selling futures. If $R(x) > p_1$, no futures contracts will be bought or sold by this individual. If, however, $R(x) \leqslant p_1$, the individual will buy or sell futures up to the limit x_h. Hence his supply curve is perfectly elastic at a futures price of F_1, and his demand curve is perfectly elastic at a futures price of F_2.

Case of a risk-loving individual
Consider the case of an individual for whom the previous assumptions apply, except that he is risk-loving in the sense that the risk he is willing to take is an increasing function of commitments in the range $0 \leqslant R(x) \leqslant 0.5$. What is the nature of his demand and supply functions for futures contracts?

As the futures price rises from μ to E_2 (Figure 7(a)), the probability of an adverse price change, for a seller, falls at a diminishing rate with respect to price. With an upward sloping linear $R(x)$ function, sales fall at a constant rate for decreases in risk. Therefore sales fall at a diminishing rate with respect to increases in price. The supply curve slopes down to the right and is concave up (Figure 9).

As the futures price falls from μ to E_1, the risk of being

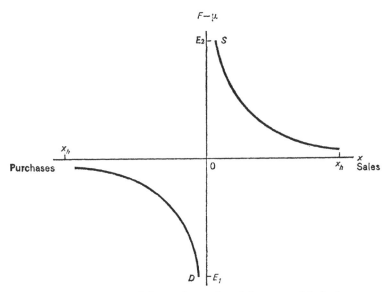

Figure 9   Demand for and supply of futures: risk-loving speculator

wrong, for a buyer, falls at a diminishing rate. With the $R(x)$ function assumed, purchases fall at a constant rate for decreases in risk. Hence purchases fall at a diminishing rate for decreases in price. The demand curve slopes down to the right and is concave down (Figure 9). In this case, the individual is partially risk-loving: he acts so that the odds are in his favour, but he increases his commitments as risk increases.

Risk premium required
It may be that the individual is inoperative for $F_4 < F < F_3$ because he requires the difference between the current

futures price and μ to be sufficient to cover a risk premium. In this case the individual's linear downward-sloping $R(x)$ function would lie in the range $0 \leqslant R(x) \leqslant p_4$. Hence his supply curve would be upward sloping, would begin at $(x = 0, F = F_3)$ and would terminate at $(x = x_h, F = E_2)$. Similarly, his downward-sloping demand curve would begin at $(x = 0, F = F_4)$ and would terminate at $(x = x_h, F = E_1)$.

If the individual's willingness to take risk is constant at $R(x) = p_4$, so that he is inoperative for $F_4 < F < F_3$, this is consistent with the interpretation that he requires the difference between F and μ to be sufficient to cover a risk premium.

Parameter changes
This method may be used to analyse changes in:

 a The individual's mean expectation
 b The dispersion of the distribution $f(E)$
 c The individual's willingness to bear risk
 d The skewness of the distribution $f(E)$
 e The price at which the individual changes from buying to selling futures
 f The individual's available capital.

The first three only of these cases will be discussed here.[4]

Increase in mean expectation[5]
Suppose that the individual's mean expectation of the spot price increases from μ to μ_1, *ceteris paribus*. Using the above assumptions, this means that at any given futures price there is a greater risk of loss for a seller, and in the case of a risk-averting individual, fewer contracts will be supplied. There is therefore a decrease in supply. On the demand side, at any given futures price, there is a lower risk of loss and hence more contracts are demanded. There is therefore an increase in demand.

In the case of a risk-loving individual (discussed above), an increase in mean expectation will obviously lead to an increase in supply and a decrease in demand. The results of a decrease in mean expectation *ceteris paribus* will be the opposite of those above.

Increase in variance

Suppose that there is an increase in the variance of the individual's distribution of expected prices, $f(E)$. The range of expectations is also assumed to increase. At any given futures price greater than μ there is an increase in seller's risk, and, for a risk-averting individual, a decrease in supply. Similarly, at any futures price less than μ there is an increase in buyer's risk, and hence a decrease in demand.

For an individual who is risk-loving in the sense discussed above, an increase in variance will clearly lead to an increase in both supply of and demand for futures contracts.

Increased willingness to bear risk [6]

Suppose that there is an increase in the individual's willingness to bear risk at any given level of commitments, although he does not act so as to have the odds against him and sells only for a futures price greater than μ. He retains a linear downward-sloping $R(x)$ function, which pivots upward on the point $(x = 0, R(x) = 0·5)$. This increased willingness to bear risk is not uniform for all levels of commitment, but is larger for higher levels than for lower levels. The result is that at any given futures price (above μ) there is an increase in supply of futures, and the maximum quantity of futures $0x_h$ is supplied at a lower price than before. Similarly, at any given futures price (below μ) there is an increase in demand, and the maximum quantity of futures $0x_h$ is demanded at a higher price.

For an individual who is risk-loving in the sense discussed above, an increased willingness to bear risk brought about by pivoting the $R(x)$ function upward on the point $(x = 0, R(x) = 0)$, will obviously lead to a decrease in supply and to a decrease in demand.

To avoid any ambiguity for a price $F = \mu$, it must be assumed that the demand and supply curves do not coincide with the horizontal axis, but that each is asymptotic to Ox.

Market equilibrium with homogeneous expectations

The aim of this section is to find the futures price and the quantity of futures contracts traded in a market with speculators only, where expectations are assumed identical for all individuals. It will be shown that homogeneity of expectations is no bar to speculative trading (as is sometimes said [7]), provided that certain other conditions are fulfilled.

The following additional assumptions are made for this section:

a That all individuals have identical subjective probability distributions of expected spot prices, of the type discussed above

b That the capital constraint x_h is identical for all individuals

c That there are no external economies or diseconomies of buying or selling futures, so that market supply and demand at any given futures price are the sum of quantities supplied and demanded by individuals respectively

d That the market is competitive.

It is clear at the outset that if expectations and willingness to bear risk are each identical for all individuals there will be no trading. The reason for this is that under such conditions there can be no price range for which both buyers and sellers exist. It can be shown, however, that homogeneity of expectations is no bar to trading if willingness to bear risk is heterogeneous. Two cases only will be discussed: first a market comprising individuals whose willingness to bear risk is a diminishing function of commitments, and second,

95

where willingness to bear risk is an increasing function of commitments for all individuals.

Case 1

Suppose that all individuals are of the risk averting type discussed above. Let us assume also:

    a That E_m, the price at which the individual changes from buying to selling, varies between individuals

    b That the series Em_i (the dividing line for the *i*th seller) is evenly spaced within the range E_1E_2;

i.e. as the futures price rises, new sellers appear at a constant rate with respect to price.

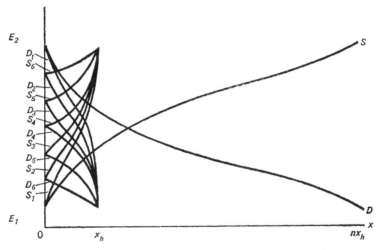

Figure 10   Market equilibrium: risk-averting speculators: expectations homogeneous, attitude to risk heterogeneous

Assumption (*a*) implies that the $R(x)$ functions exist in different ranges for different individuals, and that, except for the individual for whom $E_m = \mu$, individuals have different $R(x)$ functions for buying and selling.

It is clear that market supply will be an increasing function of the futures price, because as the price rises each seller supplies more, and more individuals become sellers. Similarly, as the price falls each buyer demands more, and more individuals become buyers. Consequently market demand is a decreasing function of price. In this case a single equilibrium, stable in both the Marshallian and Walrasian senses, will exist (from the assumptions, the equilibrium price is μ). (See Figure 10 drawn for six individuals, for illustration purposes only.)

Case 2
Suppose that all individuals are partially risk-loving in the sense discussed above. Otherwise the assumptions are as in Case 1. On the assumptions, market supply may be an increasing or a decreasing function of price. As the futures price rises more individuals become sellers, but each seller supplies less. Similarly, market demand may be an increasing or a decreasing function of price, because as price falls more individuals become buyers, but each buyer demands less. This case is shown in Figure 11, where, for purposes of illustration, the functions are drawn for six individuals only. In this instance one equilibrium only occurs and this is stable in the Marshallian sense, but unstable in the Walrasian sense. It is clear that if the second assumption in Case 1 above is relaxed, then no equilibrium may occur, or alternatively one or more equilibria may occur and these may each be stable or unstable in the above senses.

In this system there are two main senses in which an individual may be risk-loving: first, his willingness to take risk may be an increasing function of commitments; and second, he may sell futures when the price is less than E_m and buy futures when the price exceeds E_m.[8] These two senses are independent. The above method may be used to show that in a market in which individuals are risk-loving in both senses, a single equilibrium, unstable in both Marshallian and Walrasian senses, will occur. If the market is comprised of individuals who are risk-loving in the second sense but not

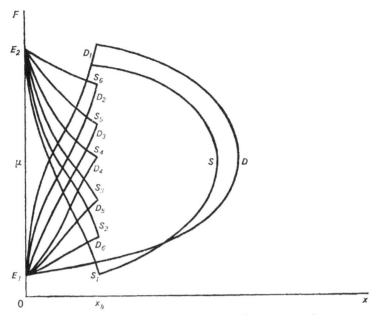

Figure 11   Market equilibrium: risk-loving speculators:
expectations homogeneous, attitude to risk heterogeneous

in the first, the above method may be used to show that the outcome will be similar to that of Case 2 above.

Thus homogeneity of expectations is no bar to speculative trading provided that willingness to take risk is heterogeneous, although equilibrium need not occur in all cases.

Market equilibrium with heterogeneous expectations

The aim of this section is, first, to find a probability density function to represent the expectations of the whole market, where individual's expectations are heterogeneous. Assume initially that we are concerned with a set of individuals' subjective probability distributions of expected spot prices which are symmetrical and have the same dispersion but different means. Suppose also that these distributions are numerous and tightly packed with uniform density in the

98

range E_3E_4. That is, the means of these distributions all lie in the range E_3E_4, and their maxima approximate a straight line. Such a set of individual distributions can be approximated by the rectangular distribution which is given by $g_0(E) = 1/(E_4 - E_3)$. Similarly, another set of individuals' distributions each with the same dispersion σ_j^2 ($>\sigma_i^2$) but with different means located in the range E_3E_4 can, under the same assumptions, be represented by the rectangular distribution $g_1(E) = 1/(E_4 - E_3)$; and so on.

Suppose, then, that the whole market set of expectations consists of individuals' distributions which differ only as regards mean and variance. Each set of individuals' distributions with the same variance but different means lying in the range E_3E_4 can be approximated by a rectangular distribution. Therefore, the whole set of market expectations can be approximated by a series of rectangular distributions $g_0(E), g_1(E), g_2(E), \ldots g_n(E)$, located within the range E_3E_4. A rectangular distribution, however, is fully specified once the range is known. Therefore $g_0(E) = g_1(E) = \ldots = g_n(E) = 1/(E_4 - E_3)$. On these assumptions, the whole set of market expectations can be approximated by the rectangular distribution $g(E) = 1/(E_4 - E_3)$.

Such a rectangular distribution has two main advantages. First, it is an approximation to any set of individuals' distributions, irrespective of their form (normal, binomial, hypergeometric), provided there is a large number packed with uniform density within a given range. The rectangular distribution can then be seen as a distribution of the individual means μ_i (it could also be seen as a distribution of the individual modes or medians), and the individual variances become irrelevant, as do the other characteristics of the individual distributions (for the purpose of defining the market expectation). The second advantage of the rectangular distribution is that the errors, where the individual $f_i(E)$ overlap the ordinates at E_3 and E_4, cancel each other out in the sense that they do not affect the mean of $g(E)$.

99

It is now possible to speak of *the expectation* of the market, and of the spread of market expectations in a precise sense. The former is given by the mean of $g(E)[= \frac{1}{2}(E_4 + E_3)]$; the latter is given by the variance of $g(E)[= \frac{1}{12}(E_4 - E_3)^2]$; (ignoring the extent to which the individual $f_i(E)$ overlap the ordinates at E_3 and E_4). So for the purpose of representing the expectations of the market by a rectangular distribution it is not necessary to assume that the individual distributions are known. It is necessary only that some measure of central value exists for each individual, and that this series is large and evenly distributed in the range $E_3 E_4$.

The question is then: What is the form of the market demand and supply functions for futures contracts when expectations are heterogeneous, and willingness to take risk is homogeneous? Two cases only will be discussed. In addition to the assumptions made in the earlier part of this section, let us assume that at any given futures price the individual estimates the probability that the price will rise or fall. If we further assume that all individuals are of the risk-averting type discussed on pp. 87–90, we can deduce that market supply is an increasing function of price (as the futures price rises, each seller supplies more, and more individuals become sellers), and that market demand is a decreasing function of price (as the price falls, each buyer demands more, and more individuals become buyers). Hence an equilibrium which is stable in the Walrasian and Marshallian senses exists.

On the other hand, if it is assumed that all individuals are partially risk-loving in the sense discussed on pp. 91–2 (sells if $F > \mu$, but $\partial R(x)/\partial x > 0$) then the market demand and supply functions may each be an increasing or decreasing function of price (as the price rises, more individuals become sellers, but each seller supplies less; as the price falls, more individuals become buyers, but each buyer demands less). Hence zero, one or more equilibria may exist and these may be stable or unstable. To derive the market demand and supply curves precisely it is necessary to know the details of the individual distributions; the market functions can then be derived as for the case of homogeneous expectations (pp. 95–8).

It can now be seen that very similar results for the market may be obtained with homogeneous expectations and heterogeneous willingness to take risk, on the one hand, or with heterogeneous expectations and homogeneous willingness to take risk on the other. Heterogeneity of both makes no difference to the general nature of the result. Homogeneity of both is a bar to trading and thus to equilibrium.

The more realistic case, where the individual μ_i are not evenly distributed in the range E_3E_4 but are clustered about a modal expectation, may be treated as a modification of the simpler case. Any clustering of individual expectations means a clustering of individual supply and demand curves, and therefore a change in the gradient of the market supply and demand curves compared with the 'rectangular' case. So the case where there is substantial agreement among speculators about what the spot price will be at the later date causes no reversal but only a modification of the previous results.

Expectations formed in terms of price spread only

Suppose that the individual forms his expectations in terms of the price spread $(F - S)$ only. The first question is what type of transaction may be undertaken? There are two main types of transaction:

'Short hedging' type of transaction

Assuming for simplicity that carrying costs are zero, and that all positions are closed out by reversal of the transaction at time t_2, the procedure for this type of transaction would be:

H   101

At time t_1: Buy spot at price S_1
      Sell futures at price F_1
At time t_2: Sell spot at price S_2
      Buy futures at price F_2
      Profit $= (S_2 - S_1) + (F_1 - F_2)$
           $= (F_1 - S_1) - (F_2 - S_2)$.

That is, a profit is realized if contango falls, or if backwardation increases.

'Long hedging' type of transaction

The procedure for this type of transaction is assumed to be:

At time t_1: Sell spot at price S_1. (This activity is constrained by the quantity of spot held by the individual.)[9]
      Buy futures at price F_1.
At time t_2: Buy spot at price S_2.
      Sell futures at price F_2.
      Profit $= (S_1 - S_2) + (F_2 - F_1)$
           $= (S_1 - F_1) - (S_2 - F_2)$.

That is, a profit is realized if backwardation falls or if contango increases.

These are not really hedging transactions, since the aim is an uncertain profit and the trader is backing his expectations (see below). The above formulae apply only where the ratio of spot to futures contracts is one-to-one; this ratio, however, may vary (see below).

The question is then: When are these transactions to be undertaken? Suppose that the individual's expectations are represented by the subjective probability distribution $f(E_c)$ with mean μ_c. If the current value of contango is $C_0 (> \mu_c)$ the subjective probability of a rise in contango is ρ_0, which we assume is less than the probability of a fall, $(1 - \rho_0)$. If the individual is of the risk-averting type discussed above, he will undertake the 'short hedging' type of transaction. If, however, the current contango is C_1 and the subjective probability of a rise in contango is ρ_1, which we assume exceeds the probability of a fall $(1 - \rho_1)$, then the 'long hedging' type of transaction is expected to be more profitable.

We have assumed the individual's willingness to take risk is a decreasing function of commitments. The question is how the quantity on the horizontal axis is to be interpreted. Must spot and futures contracts be dealt in according to a one-for-one ratio as in Leland Johnson's theory (op. cit., p. 149)? I suggest that this is not necessary, and that the individual can deal in spot and futures according to any ratio he selects. Some ratios will be more profitable than others *ex post*, but it is not possible to say which ratios the individual regards as more profitable without knowing which price he expects to change more.

Two alternative interpretations of the x-axis appear possible:

a That a unit of x represents futures and spot in a one-for-one ratio. Other ratios, however, may be more profitable.

b If the individual has expectations of which price will change by a greater absolute amount (without having an expectation of the *level* of that price), then he can specialize partly or completely in one contract. It may be possible to draw a function which gives the relationship between the degree of certainty (range 0 to 1) with which he expects one price to change more than the other, and the ratio of spot to futures contracts in which he will deal. This function will have a negative first derivative. If he is sure that all the change in spread will come from the futures price, he will not deal in spot at all. (Only in the two limiting cases (certainty = 0, 1) is an expectation about the level of one price implied.) The less certain he is that most of the change will be in the futures price, the greater the ratio of spot to futures in his portfolio.

The x-variable may be interpreted as the total number of contracts for which the individual is committed in both markets. This interpretation may be used for all ratios of spot to futures, although if the $R(x)$ function is taken as given, this assumes that willingness to take risk does not change with a change in ratio.

The question is then whether functions corresponding to the usual supply and demand functions exist. In a diagram based on Figure 8, quadrants 1 and 4 represent short positions in futures (long in spot); quadrants 2 and 3 represent long positions in futures (short in spot). For an individual who is a risk-averter quadrants 1 and 3 only are relevant. Suppose that the individual forms expectations in terms of the price spread $(F - S)$ only, and that he deals in spot and futures in a one-for-one ratio. The individual's 'long' and 'short' curves (from the futures point of view) can be derived using the method developed on pp. 89–91; the 'short' curve would have the shape of the supply curve (Figure 8), and the 'long' curve would follow the demand curve.

If all individuals form expectations of this kind, the equilibrium spread for the market will be determined by the intersection of the aggregate 'long' and 'short' curves (assuming heterogeneity of expectations and/or willingness to bear risk, as above). The total number of contracts dealt in will be known, but the actual price level will not be determined. Some additional factors must then be introduced to determine the level of one of the prices. For example, merchandising in the spot market which determined the level of the spot price would meet this requirement. The price spread, and consequently the level of the futures price, will be determined in the futures market by the actions of speculators only.

Simultaneous determination of spot and futures prices

To close off the model, and to determine spot and futures prices, a technique based on the previous section will be

104

used. In order to treat the problem in a simple way, two markets only are distinguished: the market for spot contracts and that for futures contracts.

Four categories of operator are defined: speculators, hedgers, merchants and producers. 'Speculators' are assumed to form their expectations in terms of the price spread only, and are assumed to deal in spot and futures contracts in a one-for-one ratio. It is further assumed that both expectations and willingness to take risk are heterogeneous as between individuals. It follows that both 'long' and 'short' functions will exist, as derived in the previous section.

'Hedgers' are defined as traders who enter the futures market in order to cover spot market commitments: they are therefore 'pure hedgers' in the Peston–Yamey sense. It is assumed that hedgers do not back their expectations; in so far as they do under- or over-hedge they are included in the 'speculator' category. Hedgers, who are assumed to be net short, will deal in spot and futures contracts in a one-for-one ratio. Although covering a spot market commitment, however, their market position will not be unresponsive to the price spread. We can assume that the number of spot and futures units dealt in by hedgers will be an increasing function of contango. This relationship may be derived on the behavioural assumption that hedgers determine their market position by equating contango with the marginal net cost of storage, which is itself assumed to be an increasing function of stocks.[10] This relationship is represented by the function H. The total number of spot and futures units forthcoming from the 'short' side of the (futures) market, as a function of the price spread, is given by the summation of the 'short' and H functions, resulting in the function T.

'Merchants' are long speculators in spot, and are thus merchants in the Peston–Yamey sense. Both expectations and willingness to take risk can be regarded as heterogeneous between individual merchants, and it is assumed that all are

105

risk-averting in the sense of having $\partial R(x)/\partial x < 0$. The demand function for spot contracts for this group can be derived in the way described on pp. 89–90.

'Producers' are assumed to have a conventional, positively sloped market supply function P, for spot contracts; hence this model is not subject to the restriction of a fixed stock.[11]

The equilibrium price spread is determined at b_0, by equating the 'T' and 'Long' functions. An equilibrium reached in this way will, of course, fulfil the condition established by arbitrage that $F - S \leqslant i + (c - q)$. Speculators and hedgers deal in a quantity of $0M_0$ spot contracts, and $0M_0$ futures contracts. The equilibrium spot price is determined at S_0 by equating the 'P' and 'D' functions. (Hence the level of the futures price is determined.) Producers and merchants deal in the quantity of spot contracts $0Q_0$. The quantity of spot in which hedgers and speculators deal, although forming part of the spot market transactions, will not affect the level of the spot price, since the amount of spot demanded by hedgers and 'short' speculators will be offset by the spot provided by 'long' speculators.

We are now in a position to analyse the effect of parameter shifts on the spot price and the price spread. First, suppose there is an increase in expectations: merchants revise upwards their expectations of the spot price, and speculators revise upwards their expectations of the price spread. According to the analysis on pp. 93–4, this will result in a decrease in the speculators' 'short' function and an increase in the 'long' function; there will also be an increase in demand for spot by merchants (assuming all individuals are risk-averting in the sense of having $\partial R(x)/\partial x < 0$). Hence there will be an increase in the spot price and in the price spread; the quantity of spot contracts traded, and the quantity of futures may each go either way.

Second, suppose there is an increase in the variance of expectations for both speculators and merchants. According to the method developed above, for risk-averting individuals, there will be a decrease in speculators' 'long' and 'short' functions, and a decrease in the demand for spot by merchants. Hence the spot price will fall, but the price spread may rise or fall; the quantity of spot contracts and of futures will each fall.

Third, suppose there is an increase in willingness to take risk for both speculators and merchants. Assuming that all individuals are of the risk-averting type, there will be an increase in the 'short' and 'long' functions of speculators, and in the demand for spot by merchants. This will result in an increase in the spot price, although the price spread may go either way. The quantity of spot contracts traded will increase, as will the quantity of futures.

So far it has been assumed that both speculators and hedgers deal in spot and futures in a one-for-one ratio. This assumption is perhaps too restrictive as far as speculators are concerned. In the case where speculators do not deal in spot and futures in a one-for-one ratio, and this ratio varies as between individuals, the x-axis can be taken to represent spot and futures contracts in a ratio which is a weighted average of individual ratios, and the weights are the total number of spot and futures contracts in which the individual deals. The 'hedging' and 'short' functions would then no longer be shown separately. Although pure hedgers would still deal in spot and futures in a one-for-one ratio, this would now be reflected in the distribution of individual ratios.

Notes

1 Jerome L. Stein, 'The Simultaneous Determination of Spot and Futures Prices', *American Economic Review*, vol. 51, 1961, pp. 1012–25; Stein, 'The Opportunity Locus in a Hedging Decision: A Correction', *American Economic Review*, vol. 54, 1964, pp. 762–3; M. J. Brennan, 'The Supply of Storage', *American Economic Review*, vol. 48, March 1958, pp. 50–72; L. G. Telser,

'Futures Trading and the Storage of Cotton and Wheat', *Journal of Political Economy*, vol. 66, January 1958, pp. 233–55; M. H. Peston and B. S. Yamey, 'Inter-Temporal Price Relationships with Forward Markets: A Method of Analysis', *Economica*, vol. 27, 1960, pp. 355–67; Leland L. Johnson, 'The Theory of Hedging and Speculation in Commodity Futures', *Review of Economic Studies*, vol. 27, 1959–60, pp. 139–51.

2 There is, of course, nothing new in the use of frequency distributions in micro-economics. For example, the demand curve for cash under conditions of heterogeneous but single-valued expectations described by J. Tobin, 'Liquidity Preference as Behaviour Towards Risk', *Review of Economic Studies*, vol. 25, 1957–8, p. 69 is, in fact, an ascending cumulative frequency distribution of cash held at each hypothetical interest rate. Tobin goes on to analyse the individual's demand for bonds and hence cash using two parameters (mean and standard deviation) of the individual's subjective probability distribution of return on a portfolio. The individual is assumed to select his market position so as to maximize expected utility.

Again, G. L. S. Shackle, *Decision Order and Time* (Cambridge University Press, 1961), shows that the market demand curve for bonds can be represented by the ascending cumulative frequency distribution of bonds held at each expected price, under conditions of certain expectations. He then uses his potential surprise theory to analyse market behaviour under conditions of uncertainty.

The theory developed here, however, is quite different. Although using the concept of the subjective probability distribution of expected prices, it is not an indifference curve theory, nor is it a potential surprise theory. Moreover, it addresses itself to the problem of determining the individual's position in a futures market and then to the simultaneous determination of spot and futures prices, rather than to the determination of the price of bonds.

3 In a recent questionnaire survey of twenty-five traders (Floor Members and Associate Members) on the Sydney Wool Futures Market, fourteen respondents said that their willingness to take risk was a decreasing function of commitments; the remainder replied that their willingness to take risk was constant with respect to commitments. The results of this survey will be discussed in a forthcoming paper.

4 The fourth case can be analysed in the same manner as the

second; the fifth case is dealt with on pp. 96–8; and the final case obviously causes an extension (for an increase in capital) or truncation (for a decrease in capital) of the individual's supply and demand curves. In the questionnaire survey on the Sydney Wool Futures Market (referred to above) twelve of twenty-five respondents said that the capital available for their dealings did increase. Of these two said that this would affect their dealings at all prices, five said their dealings would be affected only at high selling prices and low buying prices, while five said that their dealings would not be affected at all. (In answer to a separate question, thirteen of twenty-one respondents replied that the amount of capital available did not limit the extent of their dealing in the market.)

5 In the questionnaire survey on the Sydney Wool Futures Market, twenty-four of twenty-five respondents said that they revised their price expectations. The reasons given for revision were: State of the market (thirteen respondents), New information (eleven), State of the economy in general (eight) and Other (six). (Several respondents gave more than one reason.)

6 In the questionnaire survey on the Sydney Wool Futures Market, fourteen of twenty-three respondents said that they revised their willingness to take risk. The reasons given for revision were: State of the market (seven respondents), Record of past profits and losses (five), Psychological factors (three) and Other (three). (Several respondents gave more than one reason.)

7 For example, R. G. Hawtrey, 'Mr Kaldor on the Forward Market', *Review of Economic Studies*, June 1940, p. 205, says: 'But surely if all held the same expectations there would be no speculation.' It is clear that Hawtrey is discussing the case of multi-valued rather than single-valued (certain) expectations, for he says (p. 203), 'The most complete expectations will take the form of estimates of the respective probabilities of a series of results.' Again, when referring to 'less complete' expectations he says (pp. 203–4), 'and he need not make any estimate of the extent of the rise or fall, except that it will be considerable enough to be worth his while'.

8 There is a third sense in which an individual may be risk-loving in this system: he may act so as to have the subjective odds against him. This sense, however, is not independent. It is implied by the second sense in some cases. It is clear that an individual

who sells futures when the price is less than E_m must, for some prices, have the subjective odds against him.

9   If the individual were to sell actuals forward at time t_1, he would not be subject to this constraint. The price at which such a forward transaction would be made, however, is likely to be closer to F_1 than to S_1. See B. S. Yamey, 'Short Hedging and Long Hedging in Futures Markets: Symmetry and Asymmetry, *Journal of Law and Economics*, October 1971.

10   The marginal net cost of storage is defined in the Kaldor–Brennan–Telser tradition as being equal to $i + (c - q)$, where i = marginal interest cost, c = marginal carrying cost proper, q = marginal convenience yield. If $i, c, q > 0$, and $i', c' \geqslant 0$, and $q' < 0$ (prime markings indicate partial derivatives with respect to stocks), then $m = i + c - q \gtrless 0$ and $m' > 0$. Hence if contango is negative (backwardation) and $F - S = i + (c - q)$, then $q > i + c$; this does of course throw a substantial burden of flexibility on the marginal convenience yield.

11   Cf. Peston and Yamey, op. cit., pp. 355, 359. For the reader to whom this formulation is not acceptable, the theory developed on pp. 86–91 may be integrated with the Peston–Yamey model to determine spot and futures prices. Indeed Peston and Yamey leave the way open for this: on p. 355 n. 1 they say: 'Our objective here is . . . to present an alternative technique which is not committed to any specific theory of behaviour under uncertainty, but is sufficient for the construction of the relevant economic models.' Hence in the basic Peston–Yamey model the R function, the demand for unhedged stocks by 'merchants', which is a decreasing function of the spot price, and is unresponsive to changes in the futures price, can be derived in the way discussed on pp. 89–90. Their W function can be similarly derived. This is the demand for futures by 'speculators', which is a decreasing function of the futures price, and is unresponsive to changes in the spot price.

Questions

1 Explain the meaning of the following terms:

(a) spot price   (f) basis risk

(b) futures price   (g) over-hedge

(c) contango   (h) convenience yield

(d) spot premium   (i) risk premium

(e) maturity basis   (j) uncertain price expectations

2 What were the main generalizations about futures markets behaviour which resulted from the writings of Keynes, Hicks and Kaldor?

3 What is meant by the 'asymmetry of arbitrage'? Why does this asymmetry arise?

4 Explain the meaning, procedure and aim of 'hedging', distinguishing between 'short' and 'long' hedging. Compare the concept of hedging used by Yamey (1951) with that used by Working (1953), referring to both the motives for, and criteria of effectiveness of hedging.

5 'The conclusion in Kaldor's paper (1960) is general in the sense that it applies whether hedgers are net short or net long.' Discuss critically.

6 'Long hedging is the mirror image of short hedging in the sense that the short hedger's gain is the long hedger's loss.' Discuss critically.

7 Obtain a set of futures markets price statistics. Calculate the results for a set of hypothetical transactions using:

(a) a Yamey trading programme (*Manchester School*, 1951);

(b) a Graf trading programme (*Journal of Farm Economics*, 1953);

(c) a Gray trading programme (*Journal of Political Economy*, 1961).

What is the difference between the Gray programme and the other two?

8 'The trading programme of Roger W. Gray (*Journal of Political Economy*, 1961) is mechanical and therefore cannot be speculative.' Discuss.

9 'The concept of hedging of Holbrook Working, although more realistic than the earlier concept, does not permit one to distinguish between hedging and arbitrage.' Is this fair comment on Working? Explain.

10 Explain how equilibrium would be achieved in the Peston–Yamey model if the assumption of a fixed stock were dropped.

11 How would the conclusions of the storage models of Brennan and Telser be affected if price expectations were assumed heterogeneous?

12 'In Stein's model maximization of expected return by an individual is not the same as maximization of expected utility.' Explain.

13 Suggest how the model of J. L. Stein might be modified to take account of a risk-loving individual. Under what conditions would a corner solution result?

14 In the model of J. L. Stein, suppose there is an increase in the current futures price, *ceteris paribus*. How will this affect:

(a) the individual's supply of storage;

(b) the proportion of his stock which will be held unhedged;

(c) the quantity of hedged stock he will carry;

(d) the quantity of unhedged stock he will carry?

15 Compare the measure of effectiveness of hedging used by L. L. Johnson with that used by Truman F. Graf.

16 Suppose a trader expected a small (relative to the merchandising profit) fall in the spot price, and an equivalent fall in the futures price. What can you infer about his market position $(x_i, x_j \lessgtr 0)$ according to the analysis of L. L. Johnson?

What conditions must be fulfilled for an individual, in equilibrium, to be long in futures? Would it be possible for a trader to expect a rise in the spot price and nevertheless hold a zero position in the spot market? Explain.

17 'If price expectations are identical, there will be no trading between speculators.' Do you agree? Give reasons for your view.

Further reading

BLAU, G., 'Some Aspects of the Theory of Futures Trading', *Review of Economic Studies*, vol. 12, 1944–5, pp. 1–30.

BRENNAN, M. J., 'The Supply of Storage', *American Economic Review*, vol. 48, March 1958, pp. 50–72.

COOTNER, P. H., 'Returns to Speculators: Telser versus Keynes', *Journal of Political Economy*, vol. 68, August 1960, pp. 396–404.

COOTNER, P. H., 'Rejoinder', *Journal of Political Economy*, vol. 68, August 1960, pp. 415–18.

DOW, J. C. R., 'A Theoretical Account of Futures Markets', *Review of Economic Studies*, vol. 7, 1939–40, pp. 185–95.

GOLD, G., *Modern Commodity Futures Trading* (New York: Commodity Research Bureau, 1959).

GOSS, B. A., 'A Note on the Storage Market Equilibria of Brennan and Telser', *Australian Economic Papers*, vol. 9, 1970, pp. 273–8.

GRAF, TRUMAN F., 'Hedging—How Effective Is It?', *Journal of Farm Economics*, vol. 35, 1953, pp. 398–413.

GRAY, R. W., 'The Importance of Hedging in Futures Trading; and the Effectiveness of Futures Trading for Hedging', *Futures Trading Seminar*, vol. 1 (Madison: MIMIR, 1960).

GRAY, R. W., 'The Search for a Risk Premium', *Journal of Political Economy*, vol. 69, 1961, pp. 250–60.

GRAY, R. W., 'Why Does Futures Trading Succeed or Fail: An Analysis of Selected Commodities', *Futures Trading Seminar*, vol. III (Madison: MIMIR, 1966).

HAWTREY, R. G., 'Mr Kaldor on the Forward Market', *Review of Economic Studies*, vol. 7, 1939–40, pp. 202–5.

HICKS, J. R., *Value and Capital* (London: Oxford University Press, 1953), pp. 135–40.

HOUTHAKKER, H. S., 'The Scope and Limits of Futures Trading', in *The Allocation of Economic Resources* (Stanford University Press, 1959).

JOHNSON, L. L., 'The Theory of Hedging and Speculation in Commodity Futures', *Review of Economic Studies*, vol. 27, 1959–60, pp. 139–51.

KALDOR, N., 'Speculation and Economic Stability', *Review of Economic Studies*, vol. 7, 1939–40, pp. 1–27.

KALDOR, N., 'A Note on the Theory of the Forward Market', *Review of Economic Studies*, vol. 7, 1939–40, pp. 196–201.

KALDOR, N., 'Speculation and Economic Stability', in *Essays on Economic Stability and Growth* (London: Duckworth, 1961), pp. 17–58.

KEYNES, J. M., *A Treatise on Money*, vol. 2 (London: Macmillan, 1930), pp. 142–4.

PESTON, M. H. and YAMEY, B. S., 'Inter-Temporal Price Relationships with Forward Markets: A Method of Analysis', *Economica*, vol. 27, 1960, pp. 355–67.

REES, G. L., 'The Future of Futures', *Bankers' Magazine*, April 1965, pp. 253–60.

SNAPE, R. H. and YAMEY, B. S., 'Test of the Effectiveness of Hedging', *Journal of Political Economy*, vol. 73, 1965, pp. 540–4.

STEIN, J. L., 'The Simultaneous Determination of Spot and Futures Prices', *American Economic Review*, vol. 51, 1961, pp. 1012–25.

STEIN, J. L., 'The Opportunity Locus in a Hedging Decision: A Correction', *American Economic Review*, vol. 54, 1964, pp. 762–3.

115

TELSER, L. G., 'Futures Trading and the Storage of Cotton and Wheat', *Journal of Political Economy*, vol. 66, June 1958, pp. 233–55.

TELSER, L. G., 'Reply', *Journal of Political Economy*, vol. 68, August 1960, pp. 404–15.

TELSER, L. G. and YAMEY, B. S., 'Speculation and Margins', *Journal of Political Economy*, vol. 73, 1965, pp. 656–7.

TOBIN, J., 'Liquidity Preference as Behaviour Toward Risk', *Review of Economic Studies*, vol. 25, 1957–8, pp. 65–86.

VAILE, R. S., 'Inverse Carrying Charges in Futures Markets', *Journal of Farm Economics*, vol. 30, August 1948, pp. 574–5.

VENKATARAMANON, L. S., *The Theory of Futures Trading* (Bombay: Asia Publishing House, 1965).

WORKING, H., 'Theory of the Inverse Carrying Charge in Futures Markets', *Journal of Farm Economics*, vol. 31, February 1948, pp. 1–28.

WORKING, H., 'Futures Trading and Hedging', *American Economic Review*, vol. 43, 1953, pp. 314–43.

WORKING, H., 'Hedging Reconsidered', *Journal of Farm Economics*, vol. 35, 1953, pp. 544–61.

WORKING, H., 'Frontiers in Uncertainty Theory: The Evidence of Futures Markets', *American Economic Review*, Papers and Proceedings, vol. 51, 1961, pp. 160–93.

WORKING, H., 'New Concepts Concerning Futures Markets and Prices', *American Economic Review*, vol. 52, June 1962, pp. 431–59.

YAMEY, B. S., 'Hedging in an Organized Produce Exchange', *Manchester School*, vol. 19, 1951, pp. 305–19.

YAMEY, B. S., 'The London Metal Exchange', *Three Banks Review*, June 1956.

YAMEY, B. S., 'Short Hedging and Long Hedging in Futures Markets: Symmetry and Asymmetry', *Journal of Law and Economics*, October 1971.

For Product Safety Concerns and Information please contact our EU
representative GPSR@taylorandfrancis.com Taylor & Francis Verlag GmbH,
Kaufingerstraße 24, 80331 München, Germany

Printed and bound by CPI Group (UK) Ltd, Croydon, CR0 4YY
01/05/2025
01858369-0001